D0449116

Praise for
Relationship Wisdom:

"This book takes a variety of big topics and makes them very readable and understandable; the action steps are practical and do-able. I was left feeling at ease and optimistic. Anyone can pick up Jerilyn's book and get a great deal out of it."

~Aubrey, single

"Jerilyn has dedicated her life to being in relationships that matter. Her book is a gift to each of us who care about the people we love. I appreciate Jerilyn's willingness to share herself in this way."

~Martha, married with children

"THIS IS A GREAT BOOK! The content of this book is a wonderful resource! It's one of those books that people can pick up, instinctively turn to a page, and get an answer they're looking for that day."

~Sue, married professional

"I thoroughly enjoyed this book and see it as the cliff notes on relationships. It's easy to read one or two chapters at a time, and is filled with great insights and ideas I can use in all of my relationships."

~Peter, in a relationship, not married

Other books by Jerilyn Thiel:

Preventative Maintenance for Your Marriage – The Owner's Manual for a Couples Group (co-authored)

Relationship Wisdom

51 Tips to Enrich
Your Relationships
and
Make Life Easier

Jerilyn Thiel
Life Coach
Relationship Mentor

Copyright © 2010 Jerilyn Thiel. All rights reserved. No portion of this book may be reproduced mechanically, electronically, or by any other means, including photocopying, without written permission of the publisher. It is illegal to copy this book, post it to a website, or distribute it by any other means without permission from the publisher.

Jerilyn Thiel
Centennial, CO 80121
720-283-0532
JerilynThiel@comcast.net

www.YourPossibilities.com

Limits of Liability and Disclaimer of Warranty

The author and publisher shall not be liable for your misuse of this material. This book is strictly for informational and educational purposes.

The purpose of this book is to educate and entertain. The author and/or publisher do not guarantee that anyone following these techniques, suggestions, tips, ideas, or strategies will become successful. The author and/or publisher shall have neither liability nor responsibility to anyone with respect to any loss or damage caused, or alleged to be caused, directly or indirectly by the information contained in this book.

This book is dedicated to my husband, Greg, and my children, Amber and Tyler.

Thank you for your amazing love and your unwavering support.

Through my relationships with each of you, I have learned how to be a better me.

I love you with all my heart.

Acknowledgments and Gratitudes

To my parents, Victor and Eleanor Bergstreser (married 53 years): your example of how to ride the waves in a marriage gave me the foundation for this book. Your love for each other and for Judy, Brian, and me taught me the power of family. Thank you!

To Judy: You are my sister and my friend; I am so lucky. You are an amazing woman. I love you, I appreciate you, and I admire you.

To Brian: You are a man of integrity who sees the good in other people. I wish more people lived by your example. I love you.

Thank you to all the members of my Couples Group: Sue and Dean Liming, Brian and Stacy Burd, and Denise Imansepahi and Shawn Boyle. Our time together continues to impact my life and my relationship with Greg. I am forever grateful for your commitment to healthy relationships and your reminder to have fun.

To all of my teachers on this path of self-discovery: Each one of you appeared at the perfect time and taught me exactly what I needed, in that moment, to grow into the person I am today. Thank you for being you and for sharing your wisdom with me.

To my extended family, friends, neighbors, coworkers, and all others I encounter on this journey through life: Thank you for letting me practice my skills and figure out where I still need to grow. May each of you bask in the goodness of life over and over again.

To all my life coaching clients and workshop participants; past, present and future: Your willingness to do the work and make changes in your lives is humbling. Thank you for trusting me to support you on your journey.

And deep gratitude to all those who supported the completion of this book: Greg Thiel, for your unconditional support and countless read-throughs; Sue Liming, for your glorious red pen, your many insightful ideas, and your belief in this book; Aubrey Hill and Martha Pasternack, for your willingness to read and edit my manuscript and to support me on this journey with love. And to Donna Kozik and your team at *Write a Book in a Weekend*: because of your willingness to live your purpose, I had the chance to live mine – thank you!

Contents

❧

Section 1

Relationship Wisdom for All of Your Relationships

Section 2

Relationship Wisdom for Couples

Section 3

Relationship Wisdom for Parents

Section 4

Relationship Wisdom for Singles

A Few Helpful Thoughts about This Book

When you really think about it, relationships are the one constant in life. Not necessarily the same relationships all the time, but everywhere we go and everything we do involves relationships. We have a relationship with ourselves, relationships with our partner and our kids, relationships with extended family and friends, relationships with coworkers, and – for some, the biggest relationship of all – our relationship with God. They are a vital piece of our daily life that honestly can make a good day or a bad day. Often the difference between these two is simply how we choose to interact in these relationships.

This book has been written to give you an abundance of ideas for making your relationships work more smoothly and easily. The tips are intended to inspire you to look at relationships differently; some are designed to teach you something new, and a few were created so that we can laugh together at the oddness of being human. Like everything else in our lives, whether these tips work or not depends on if you apply the knowledge you will gain in these pages.

Every single tip is something that I use and that I teach my clients – they do work! These tips make relationships easier, more enjoyable, and more fulfilling; this also includes your relationship with yourself. I want to empower you to speak up for yourself in loving ways and to stand by your beliefs and values. The best relationships are the ones where we're not enabling each other (i.e., trying to read minds, second-guessing what the other needs, sacrificing our needs for another's), but rather where we know ourselves well enough to communicate with kindness, heal any hurts, and go after the love we want. These skills will teach and encourage you to do that.

Have fun with it – life is a journey and learning new skills is a process. Laugh when you mess up, take note of how you could have done better, and keep at it until it becomes part of who you are. You will be delighted and amazed at how much more satisfied you are with all of your relationships.

Take special note that every tip could apply to everyone – so if you're single, also read the chapters for couples and parents. If you're a couple, also read the chapter for singles. If you're challenged by extended family, friends, or coworkers, this whole book will come in handy. These tips do not have to be read in any order, so if you like to skip around, go for it.

On a personal note, I want to introduce you to my family since you'll be reading about them throughout this book. Greg and I have been married since 1990. He is a kind man who has endured my many changes over the years and has willingly come along on the journey. Our relationship has gone through different highs and lows; and yet neither one of us ever considers leaving the relationship to be an option. We use the skills I describe in this book to keep recreating and redefining our marriage, and for this I am eternally grateful. We have two kids, Amber and Tyler. Having kids is unlike anything I ever dreamed it would be – it is so much more! These two delightful and incredibly different people constantly show me where I need to make improvements, and they remind me that nothing in life is static. Family life is a constantly evolving journey. And like every part of our lives, some days are easy and some are not; what's required is a willingness to be creative and resourceful to make it work.

With great respect, I send you on your journey into this book. As you dive into the chapters ahead, stay open to the impact these skills will have on your relationships. Remember to trust yourself and enjoy learning something new.

Jerilyn

Section 1

Relationship Wisdom
for All of Your Relationships

The self is not something ready-made, but something in continuous formation through choice of action.

~John Dewey

When you blame others, you give up your power to change.

~Author Unknown

Communication is to relationships what breath is to life.

~Virginia Satir

❧ Chapter 1 ☙

Reality Check

"*If you do what you've always done, you'll get what you've always gotten.*" This quote rocked my world in 1989 and literally changed who I was at the core of my being. I was on the verge of going after the biggest, scariest goal I'd ever set for myself: self-employment. This was a different world from the one I grew up in and the one I was currently involved in - the one that contained a steady paycheck. On top of that, I had self-doubt, asking: "Who do you think you are to embark on this bold path?"

Yet I knew if I didn't make the leap, I would always regret it and I would feel like I wasn't living up to my potential. I was waffling back and forth about what to do when I walked into my bank, and this quote said the very thing I needed to hear. I vividly remember thinking, "If I am going to have the life I really want, I must be willing to do things differently." So even though I was scared and way outside my comfort zone, I quit my job. That change was one of the best things I've ever done for myself. It literally changed everything in my life for the better, because I was willing to travel down a path I'd never gone down before.

Now it's your turn: If you continue to do what you've always done in your relationships, you're going to get what you've always gotten. So where are your relationships begging for some new skills? What old "tried and true" methods are completely outdated and no longer effective? Where are you losing connections with others because you don't know how to make those connections better? It's time to start asking: "What am I going to change so my relationships can be different?"

If you want better communication, then how are *you* going to learn to communicate better or differently? If you want more depth to your connections, then what will *you* do to add that depth? If you want more acceptance, then how are *you* going to be more accepting? Basically consider anything that you want more of in your relationships – anything you want to be different, anything you want to be better – and ask yourself what *you're* going to do differently. Remember, if your life and your relationships are going to change, then it's time for *you* to change – not your partner, friends, family, kids, or coworkers – but *you*! Yes, they will most likely come along on the journey and make changes too, but the first step must be taken by *you*. Find peace with this truth and let go of whining about *why* you're the one who has to take the first step.

Remember, you're taking action because you know your life and your relationships can be better – and you want them to be better. This is an incredibly powerful place to be. It reminds you that change starts with *you*. You are not powerless to improve you life; actually, it's just the opposite – you have all the power to make your life anything you want it to be based on your willingness to do things differently. So let's not waste another minute. Pick something you want to work on and let's get moving. You'll find that the benefits of taking action far outweigh the costs.

Your Action Step: Identify a relationship in which you would like to feel more connected. Ask what it is that's stopping this connection – communication, not enough shared activities, an old hurt that needs to be forgiven, etc. – and make a plan to do something to move you in a positive direction. You could schedule a time to have a heart-to-heart conversation, or plan an activity that you know you'll both enjoy. Perhaps it's time to write a letter of forgiveness. Then remember to celebrate that you took action and got things moving.

Chapter 2

What You Focus On Expands

I live with complete conviction that *what you focus on does expand.* Focus on love; you'll experience more love. Focus on joy; you'll experience more joy. Focus on frustrations; you'll experience more frustrations.

The beginning of each day brings the daunting task of deciding whether you will live today seeing the positive or the negative aspects of your relationships. Will you dwell on the dirty dishes or remember the happy, full bellies? Will you be weighed down by responsibility or grateful for the abundance in your life? Will you focus on what your loved ones are doing wrong or what they're doing right? Here's another way to look at this topic: are you consciously choosing to build up your relationships or are you tearing them down? As Dr. Phil says, "You are either contributing to or contaminating a relationship at all times."

Yes, there are people who might argue that, while this is a nice theory, they question how to focus on the positive while still acknowledging a problem that needs to be worked on. In every relationship, there will regularly be obstacles that need to be fixed, adjusted, solved, and compromised on – the difference is where your thoughts dwell on a consistent basis. If you have a running dialogue in your head about how bad things are, you are going to find more bad things to add to the list. Instead, if you take note of something that needs fixing, set up a time to work on it and proceed to focus on more positive aspects of the person or situation; you will find you only have one issue to solve, not ten. Positive change begins with being mindful of the running dialogue in your head and not letting that dialogue spin you down a negative path.

Now is the time to seriously contemplate: are you looking for what's wrong in your relationships or are you seeing what's right and good about your relationships? Where are you focusing your *mental energy*? Remember, we can't think two thoughts at the same time, so if you're consciously feeding the positive side of life, the negative side will not have a voice, and you will find more evidence of things to be positive about.

Your Action Step: For one week, practice seeing the good in life. Think about all your blessings as you drive to work. During your day, consciously reflect on what you have to be grateful for (even keep a gratitude journal), and praise the people in your life daily for something they did well. And then, at the end of the week, take stock of how you feel and how this exercise impacted your life and your thoughts.

❧ Chapter 3 ❧

Uniquely You

I'm a very visual person and one day, during meditation, the image that appeared to me was a giant puzzle. The message that followed was incredibly clear: we are each part of a giant puzzle, and without each of us the puzzle would be incomplete.

It's time to embrace that you are unique and the world needs you. There is no one who looks exactly like you; no one who thinks exactly like you; no one who has your mannerisms, your goals, your dreams, or your passions. There is no one who has your history, no one who has had all of the experiences you have had, no one who has overcome exactly the same challenges you have overcome. Nor is there anyone who has had the exact friends and intimate relationships, or the same series of jobs in the exact order you have had. All these relationships and events have made you who you are.

You bring special skills, valuable passions, and unique wisdom to the evolution of the planet. YOU are here for a reason. And in order to fulfill your part of the greater puzzle, it is vital to honor your life exactly as it is. That doesn't mean staying stuck in bad situations or never making changes – it means remembering that you have value just because you're you.

Remember, no one else can be your piece of the puzzle and you can't be theirs. So, as you are honoring your unique path on this planet, remember that everyone else has their own unique path.

Do your best to step away from judgment of others since you really don't know the intimate details of what has unfolded or what is currently unfolding for them.

Keep in mind that, in traveling each of our unique journeys, we are never stagnant. We are each continually evolving beings. From day to day and year to year, we will be experimenting with different pieces of who we are and polishing out the rough spots. Each one of our long term relationships needs to be fluid enough that it can bend with the growth and evolution of each person within the relationship, thus honoring each person's unique piece of the greater puzzle.

Your Action Step: Write down five things that are uniquely you – things that light up your soul, things that touch others, things that make the planet a better place – and then find a way to celebrate each of them.

Chapter 4

Comparisons Wound Your Soul

How often have you compared yourself, your life, or your journey to someone else's? How often do you come up the loser when you do this? How often do you use it as a way to boost your ego and bring yourself a bit of false comfort?

Comparisons are one of the evils of our society. They completely negate the value of our uniqueness. And yet all of us have been taught to compare our bodies, our education, our income, our standard of living, our housekeeping skills, our health, our wins and losses, and just about anything else you can imagine to those of other people. When we compare, we come out less than others and diminish our self-esteem, or we come out better than others and build a false sense of worth.

Comparisons do not serve us – they wound us, deep in our soul. They take away our drive to be unique individuals and they diminish the value of others as unique individuals. We each came here with a different purpose and mission. When we waste energy comparing any part of our journey to another's, we are distracted from our powerful purpose here on planet earth – TO BE UNIQUELY OURSELVES and no one else.

Consciously take note of where and how you compare yourself to others on a daily basis. Then give yourself a gigantic gift and practice stepping away from comparisons. There will definitely be times when you fall back into those old patterns. The idea is to raise your awareness and <u>practice</u> NOT comparing who you are to anyone else, so eventually this will become your new habit. Your soul will thank you, your life will be more filled with joy, and you will be supporting the planet in getting rid of an unnecessary and debilitating evil.

Your Action Step: Take an introspective inventory. Write down all the ways you compare yourself to others. Spend a few days really noticing how and where comparisons show up. Then make a commitment to yourself that, for one day, you are going to stop any and all comparisons as soon as you hear them in your head or coming out of your mouth. Once you become aware of a comparison, change it to something positive. Notice at the end of the day how that experience changed you – and recommit to doing it again and again and again.

๑ Chapter 5 ๖

The Four Components of Connection

Life is a constant series of relationships. Everywhere we go, everything we do involves a relationship of some kind. Relationships are the lifeline, the soul, the meat of our existence. An intimate piece of making relationships work is understanding what it is that draws us to one person and not another, gaining clarity about why some people stay in our lives longer than others, or learning what makes a relationship seem easy with one person but not another.

In every relationship, we are connecting to others primarily through one of the four components of connection:

- Physical – activities that engage and involve the body: energy levels (high-energy person vs. couch potato) and physical contact (hugs, sex, affection, touch).

- Mental – activities that engage the brain and create left brain stimulation, the thinker in us: work, education, current events, crossword puzzles, etc.

- Emotional - activities that engage the right side of the brain including feelings and emotions. This is where extended family would fit if the only connection with them is the emotional attachment to your shared history.

- Spiritual – activities that connect us to the inner journey of who we are: religion, spirituality, core values, nature.

In order for each of us to feel and experience our life to the fullest, we must be clear about which kinds of connections we crave the most, which ones make us feel the most alive, and which ones satisfy us the most. Connecting with people who enjoy the same kinds of things we do, being realistic about people's limits, and being honest with ourselves around these four elements of connection automatically support healthier relationships.

Stop in this moment and think of things you love to do. Think of times when you are engaged in the moment, full of life, vibrant, passionate, happy, content, and focused. These activities most likely tie to your primary connection need. Keep in mind that, while an activity or event may overlap into more than one connection category, often the intention of an activity is aimed at fulfilling one primary connection need.

An example might be hiking with a friend. Do you enjoy hiking with a friend because it satisfies primarily a physical, an emotional, or a spiritual need? For me, hiking is all about the spiritual fulfillment I get from nature – the physical benefit and the emotional connection are just added extras. What about a book club? Did you join primarily for the mental connection of reading and discussing the book, or for the emotional connection of being with friends? What about sex? Is that primarily physical for you, or is it more emotional?

As you gain clarity on what meets your deepest needs, it becomes easier to find people, situations, activities, and events that will fill you up, leaving you with a greater sense of satisfaction and wholeness.

Your Action Step: Write down 10 to 20 things you really enjoy – things that are incredibly satisfying to you. Beside each item, write down the primary connection need it satisfies and then any additional connection needs it meets. Now, take note of what your connection needs are in order, from one through four; one being the need that is vital for your happiness and sense of well being, and four being the need that you maybe don't specifically seek out every day. This is the information that will serve you in making and keeping more solid relationships.

Chapter 6

Creating More Fulfilling Relationships

Self-knowledge will always support healthier relationships. With the information you uncovered in the previous chapter about what your most important connection needs are and which needs are lower than others, you can begin to find people and activities that will ensure a happier, healthier you.

My two highest categories are spiritual connection and emotional connection. The other two, physical and mental, are still vital in helping me to be a well-rounded person, but they aren't as critical to my daily personal fulfillment. I typically find my relationships much more satisfying if I bring in people who also enjoy a spiritual and/or emotional connection. My best friends are the ones who can sit with me and talk for hours over coffee. The times I feel most valued by Greg are when he listens to me. Taking time to connect with God each day is also critical for me.

Another gift in knowing this information is being aware of where people fit in your life and releasing expectations that they'll be anything else to you. Perhaps you have a friend that you love to go skiing with, but you really don't have a lot to talk about. Why not just enjoy this person as your ski buddy and not expect anything more? What about family? Perhaps your only connection with them is through your history – nothing wrong with that – and maybe it's time to let go of hoping it will be anything more. How about your coworker? Maybe you two do great at the office bouncing ideas off of each other and meeting deadlines, but outside of the office there is really nothing you would enjoy doing together. Putting these relationships into perspective frees you to find new connections, and frees other people from being something they're not.

Applying this to a committed partnership will allow both of you to see where you can build on the relationship strengths and where you might need to branch out for greater life satisfaction. Become aware of the areas in which you and your partner have a wonderful time together – the things you do well, things you enjoy, things that seem to flow easily. This points to similar areas of connection for both of you and can often meet two different connection needs. For many men, sex is primarily about the physical connection; for women, it's about the emotional connection – the same activity meets both of your needs in different ways. This can happen with a variety of activities, so explore each other's connection needs and see what activities you enjoy together that fill you both up. Then be aware of areas you might need to expand beyond your partnership to feel greater life satisfaction. Just remember to keep the boundaries of your partnership in place as you explore new ways to get your connection needs met so that you continue to build up the relationship, not tear it down.

Keep in mind that we all want to connect – it's human nature. So don't fight your connection needs. Honor them. And don't judge one connection component as being better than another – we are all different, so the ways we connect will be different. Look for new and creative ways to fulfill your connection needs and notice how much more satisfied you are.

The added benefit to understanding and applying the awareness of your connection needs is that an internally satisfied person is much easier to be in a relationship with.

Your Action Step: Answer the following questions with as much detail as possible:

- What are my highest connection needs?

- How do I best meet those connection needs? With whom?

- Are there more people I can bring into my life to support me in meeting my connection needs?

- What other activities do I want to incorporate to meet my connection needs?

- Are there any people in my life who are really good in one area, but don't quite cut it in another area? Can I be real and honest with myself about this and lower my expectations for this person?

- How does this information support my current relationships?

- How will I use this information from today forward?

Chapter 7

Patience and Kindness

I once heard it said that patience and kindness are the bookends of love. Love is such a beautiful word – such an amazing feeling. Love is a precious gift we give to each other; it is a way we express and share ourselves as human beings. Most of the time, love is so rich and full that words truly don't do it justice. Love comes from the inside; it bubbles up, flows over, and touches others in special ways.

Love can also be very slippery. Have you ever noticed that those we say we love the most are the ones we often treat the worst? We take our loved ones for granted. Sadly, we often do these things without conscious thought. That's where patience and kindness become a way to change and experience greater love.

You have most likely heard the scripture, "love is patient, love is kind." Think of patience as the preventive measure – when you are patient with your loved ones, you are less likely to react to their shortcomings. You are exercising self-control and essentially diverting a potential problem.

Kindness is the other bookend. Kindness is proactive. It means taking clear and decisive steps to be loving. These are the moments when you give of yourself through your time, your talents, or your treasures. Think of kindness as a way to build up the love between you and others.

So, we have patience on one end and kindness on the other – it's easy to imagine love living between them. Who doesn't want to be around someone who is patient with them, or who expresses kindness without conditions on a regular basis? What better way to show your love than to practice patience and kindness and see what blooms?

I also invite you to think much bigger than just those you are in close relationships with. Think of the grocery store clerk, the customer service representative, a coworker – anyone with whom you run short on patience and kindness. You will have an opportunity to impact another human being in a positive way when you use these two skills as a backdrop for all your interactions.

Your Action Step: First, become aware of where and with whom you are running short on patience and kindness. Next, challenge yourself to practice being more patient and kind, and see what magical things unfold. How do you feel? How are people responding to you? What's different in your world?

❧ Chapter 8 ❧

Communication Builders

Many of us have either heard or have said the words "We NEED to talk!" These are words that set up our partner/kids/friends/colleagues to enter a conversation bracing for the worst, with defenses ready and energy on high alert. Stop and ask yourself: "Can someone really listen to me if they are preparing their defense for the attack they think they are about to receive?"

The answer is NO, so here are five skills that will help your conversations go much more smoothly:

- Prefacing – this is the set up tool. Give the recipient a clue about what's coming in a gentle manner. "I have something important to discuss with you. When would be a good time for us to talk?" This skill will give both parties time to emotionally prepare for important conversations. (See Chapter 9 for more information on prefacing.)

- Tone of voice and body language – people don't listen very well when someone is using a stern tone of voice, intensely focusing their eyes, or crossing their arms. Practice softening your tone, your facial features, and your physical posture – any area of your body that is tense and in a fighting stance.

- Dialogue vs. lecturing – engage the recipient, talk with

them, give them a little bit of information; and allow space for them to process, ask questions, or give their thoughts. For our family, there is almost nothing that shuts down discussions faster than the feeling of being talked at.

- Assumptions – don't make any! It's easy to think you know why someone did whatever they did or how they're going to respond to something you did. Be willing to throw all your assumptions out the window and be fully present in the conversation as it unfolds.

- See that the other person's uniqueness has value – this helps us remember that the person we are engaging in conversation has their own history and skills. They are not intentionally (except in very rare cases) wanting to hurt us. They really are doing the best they can, and we have to work together to find common ground.

As you practice these skills, know that some days it will be easy and some days it may be more challenging. Building healthy communication skills takes the awareness of where you can improve, the willingness to keep trying, and the courage to admit your mistakes.

Your Action Step: For today, practice one of the above skills; for instance, try using a prefacing statement or take note of your body language and adjust accordingly. Tomorrow, practice another one, and continue until all five communication-builders have been applied to your life on a regular and consistent basis.

Chapter 9

Starting a Conversation Off On the Right Foot

Prefacing is the single most effective tool Greg and I use in our marriage. We have used it since we learned it, and have never regretted starting a conversation this way.

It's the lead-in, the setup, the attention-getter, and the way to clearly ask for what you need. It alerts your partner – or anyone you're talking to – as to the importance of the conversation and your emotions around it so there aren't any surprises. It also shows that you respect them enough not to blindside them, and it clarifies a time to talk in the near future so everyone can be fully present in what is being discussed.

We have also found that it sparks a bit of natural curiosity. It doesn't matter if you have set up the conversation for a few minutes away or even days away – the other person begins to wonder what might be discussed and is usually more eager to hear what's going on.

Here is a sampling of possible prefacing statements:

- "I have something really important to talk to you about; when would be a good time?"
- "I did something and I'm scared to tell you; when can we talk? And please, I need you to just listen first and try to have compassion."

- "I'm really upset and need to talk to you. Is this a good time, or when would be a better time for you?"

Often when I use one of the above statements, Greg's first question is: "Did I do something wrong?" Occasionally the answer is yes and I tell him *briefly* what it was so he can prepare for our talk. Many times the answer is no and, by him asking this one question, he can relax and open his mind and be ready to support me. This has been so powerful for our relationship and it has defused many potential fights before they started.

Here are more prefaces geared toward many different subjects and people:

- "Kids – Dad and I have something to discuss at dinner." (This just prepares them to come to the table ready to talk – and remember, it stirs curiosity, so at least for a while you will have their full attention.)

- "This weekend, when we're in the mountains (at the beach, sitting on the deck), could we take an hour to talk about ____?"

- "I have a big project at work coming up and I need to talk about how this will impact my schedule and the family. When would you like to do this?"

- "John, your performance review is tomorrow. Please come prepared to tell me three things you think you've done really well this year and two things you know you need to work on."

- "I have some big expectations around how tonight might go. Is this a good time to share them with you? If not, when would be a better time?"

- "We're having this huge party and I'd like to talk about what kind of help I'll need and my timeline for getting things done. Would later this evening work for you?"

- "My mother is coming for a long visit and I would like

us all to discuss how to make it fun for everyone. When would you like to do this?"

- "I would like us to take a closer look at our finances. Do you have time on Saturday morning? If not, when do you have time?"

- "I can only imagine how hard _____ has been on you. When could we talk about how I can support you?"

- "I'm a bit embarrassed to share this with you. Are you in a good space to listen or shall I share later?"

There are as many variations of prefacing statements as there are people, so practice and find what works best in your situations.

Your Action Step: Write down three ways in which you might preface a difficult conversation. Then practice one this week and take time to reflect how it supported the relationship.

Chapter 10

Talk, Accept, or Distance

There are some relationships that are always going to push your irritation buttons. I call these people "the ones that come with the package": coworkers, in-laws, neighbors, extended family. These are people you maybe didn't choose to have in your life, but for whatever reason you really can't throw them out either. So how do you make these relationships work when you aren't really invested in them?

You have three choices:

1. Have an open (perhaps heart-to-heart) conversation with them – maybe many conversations. Use the skills in this book and other relationship books to feel confident and ready to be really honest with them. Share your truth and ask them to share theirs. Be willing to find a middle ground to whatever is bothering you.

2. Accept them exactly as they are and don't expect anything to be any different. This one comes in really handy for extended family. You aren't going to change them and you may not see them often enough to have a heart-to-heart conversation with them, so it's time to accept them. Think about holidays with extended family. What if you showed up being completely accepting of the fact that cousin Bob is going to give you a big hassle about your career path (oh well, you like your career) or Aunt Betty is going to grill you about your social life (maybe

she just wants to know what's going on). Imagine being emotionally prepared and detached enough so that, when these conversations come up, you could simply chuckle inside and then find the perfect opportunity to change the subject. It will certainly make for much more enjoyable gatherings.

3. Distance yourself from these people. If the situation is so bad that you can't have a conversation and you just can't accept their behavior, then another choice is to distance yourself. This doesn't have to be a bad thing. It can simply be a choice that supports who you really want to be on this planet. (When I distance myself from someone, it's because I don't like how I show up around this person or how I feel after an interaction with this person – it's just not healthy, and I'm a better person if I distance myself from them.)

A key to making this process work is to do it with kindness, confidence, and peaceful detachment. This means you are acting in your own best interest without making anyone wrong.

Your Action Step: The next time you're around people you didn't necessarily invite into your life and the irritation starts in your stomach, ask yourself which of these three tactics would really serve you and the relationship the best.

❧ Chapter 11 ❧

Reminders for Disagreements

D isagreements are part of life. They're going to happen, so there is no sense in trying to avoid them. Practice making them less destructive and painful. Here are a few tips to minimize the damage of a disagreement:

- Please don't expect people to read your mind. Tell them clearly, concisely, and responsibly what's going on.

- Tackle challenges one issue at a time. Start with the pressing issue that is up for you in the moment. If you find that more than one issue is starting to surface then "bottom-line" it – what is really at the core of all these issues that you want to deal with? It could be that you aren't feeling connected. Maybe you need more help than you've been getting. Maybe you're tired and feel completely overwhelmed.

- Leave the past in the past. I recognize that some issues are too big to apply this to, and in those cases I highly recommend seeing a qualified professional to help you come to terms with the past. Otherwise, leave the past in the past. When you argue with your partner, your kids, or even your friends, don't use this as an opportunity to keep digging up old stuff. Deal with what's present – and only what's present.

- Bad moods are part of life, but don't sling them all over everyone. Sometimes we all wake up cranky. Or things happen during the day and we're just mad. It's normal to feel this way sometimes; it's part of being human. But if we're not careful, we can also be cruel. So if you're having a bad day, own it – don't fling it everywhere you go or use it as an opportunity to pick a fight. Personally, if I'm having a bad day, I have as little interaction with others as possible until I've worked it through. Sometimes it even supports me to find someone neutral to talk to. Be healthy with your bad moods and they won't be so bad.

Sometimes it is through our disagreements that we learn the most about ourselves and those around us. Once you have moved through the disagreement, reflect on how you showed up and pay attention to how the other person showed up. What did you learn about yourself and the other person? What do you want to do differently next time? What triggered the disagreement, and can that be circumvented next time? Remember to use the information from the "I'm Sorry" and Forgiveness chapters (15 & 16) to move forward.

Your Action Step: Take a minute to think about how you usually handle disagreements. Then decide how you'd like to show up differently next time. Come up with two or three specific behaviors you want to do differently, write them down, and keep your list handy. Notice how using these healthier choices create new outcomes from previous disagreements.

Chapter 12

Disappointments

There are several givens when it comes to relationships: if you are loving, you will be loved; if you practice these relationship skills, you will see changes; and there will be times of disappointment in every relationship.

I wish it wasn't true – I wish you were never disappointed in your relationships. I wish people would never let you down. I wish whatever you needed would always be fulfilled by others.

Unfortunately, it isn't possible to avoid disappointment, so it is better to be keenly aware of this than to be blindsided when it happens. Often we are disappointed because people are making a choice that goes against what we had hoped they would choose. So I may be disappointed when my friend is not available to listen to me, or I may be disappointed when Greg has a different perspective on things, or I may be disappointed when it seems I don't matter to someone.

It doesn't feel good, but it happens. And it happens because people are wrapped up in their own worlds, taking care of their own needs, and doing the best they can. We have no idea what kind of stress makes them unavailable, or what kind of chatter is going on in their head that keeps them from listening to us, or what magnitude of things they want to accomplish in the day that keeps them from saying yes to our requests. It can hurt and it can add extra burden to our lives, but in most cases people don't disappoint us on purpose; they disappoint us because they are working to be true to themselves.

The other fact that warrants a reminder here is that we have all disappointed others as well. It has happened in the past, and it will happen in the future. Simply through our daily interactions and others' expectations of us, disappointments will arise. How you handle the disappointment that others feel can make all the difference. This could be as simple as validating their feelings and not making them wrong, or it could mean being willing to compromise on the issue at hand.

One important thing to consider is *how often* others are disappointed in you and *how often* others disappoint you. If it happens regularly in your relationships, then there could be a bit of selfish behavior going on that warrants further investigation. If it only happens occasionally, then you are probably in balance and this is just a moment of clashing needs.

Your Action Step: Next time you feel disappointed, ask yourself these questions: "What was I wanting from this person?" "What other healthy and respectful ways can I get this need met?" "Where in my life am I currently disappointing others?" Many times, what happens to us is also being projected from us. Be willing to look at how you're disappointing others and clean this up.

❧ Chapter 13 ❧

Passive-Aggressive Behavior and Guilt Trips

Passive-aggressive behavior and guilt trips use up vital amounts of emotional energy and, quite frankly, are a big waste of time. These are games people play in relationships instead of being honest or taking the time to figure out what's really happening.

Passive-aggressive behavior is a defensive pattern that manifests in negative ways. It shows up in fault-finding, moodiness, sulkiness, temper outbursts, procrastination, stubbornness, and resentment. (There may be more symptoms, so if you need additional information, contact a qualified therapist.) Perhaps it's time to begin handling your relationships in a healthier manner; instead of being moody around your partner and hoping they'll figure out why, tell him or her why you're upset. Instead of telling someone all the things they're doing wrong, try to be clear on what you're really needing and just ask for it. We waste so much time dancing around the heart of a matter because we are afraid of what will happen if we tell the truth. In doing this, we are losing our connections. Instead, use a prefacing statement, tell the truth, and see what unfolds.

Here's an example of how I get passive-aggressive. I have a tendency to get irritable (i.e., moody and resentful at the same time); when I'm like this, no one enjoys being around me and it's not productive. Yet if I will simply take one minute and ask myself what's going on and what am I needing right now – and then go do that – I am a much happier person. The odd thing is, when I'm irritable, all I usually need is a few minutes alone – that's not a lot to ask and no one in my family would deny me that. Yet it is my fear of letting others down and the personal pressure I put on myself that can easily stop me from taking those few minutes.

Guilt trips are another relationship saboteur. Have you ever heard, "If you loved me you'd ___" or "I work so hard – why can't you do ___"? These are no fun to receive, so why do we dish them out? Basically, guilt trips are used as a way to play into other people's sense of obligation. Yet by doing this, what we're really creating is a division in our relationship. The next time you have the urge to lay a guilt trip on someone to get them to help you, try telling them the truth. It may not be the easiest thing you do this year, but you will begin to have healthier, more connected relationships if you do.

Your Action Step: For the next week, pay close attention to any passive-aggressive behaviors and urges to lay guilt trips. Notice what's triggering these defensive patterns and ask yourself what's really going on. Seek to find a healthier way to respond.

Chapter 14

Integrity Builds Trust

Integrity is a cornerstone of relationships. It builds trust, creates safety, and tears down walls. Integrity is an internal alignment system that says, "What I think, say, and do matches my beliefs and my values."

One of my values is kindness. I believe it's one of the most precious things we do for each other and one of the best ways we connect. So if this is a value of mine, then how are my thoughts showing up? What about my words and my actions – do they tell the world that kindness matters to me? Now, I fully own that I have my bad days and it may seem that I'm not being very kind. When that happens, the key to standing in integrity is being aware that something unkind has occurred and having the willingness to making amends.

How are you doing in the area of integrity? Are you a person who walks your talk? Are you someone who treats people the same whether they're in the room or out of the room? Are you someone who keeps their word? Are you someone who wants to believe in good things but is constantly in a grumpy mood? Do you say that you respect your kids but then never listen to them?

When you look at your own integrity, evaluating your shortcomings is not a reason to beat yourself up for the times you've fallen short, but rather an opportunity to make new choices. At these times, pause and evaluate who it is that you want to be, and then consciously and deliberately make changes to be that person. Take note of situations which can easily push you into old "out of integrity" behaviors (for me, it's people who gossip) and go into those situations mentally armed with how you're going to stay aligned with your beliefs and your values. (I have worked on creating graceful but direct ways to change the subject when people start gossiping.)

Developing integrity is a continually evolving process. Every time we learn something new about ourselves or go through a rough period in life, we are faced with the opportunity to evaluate our integrity and make changes where necessary. My personal mission is to continue exploring what integrity means to me, really thinking about how it shows up in my daily life; and to be aware – physically, mentally and emotionally – when I'm out of integrity. Remember, like all of the skills in this book, integrity is a choice. The payoff for being a person of integrity means that, at the end of the day, you can be satisfied with how you showed up and you can go to sleep at night with a clean conscience.

Your Action Step: Take note of where and how your thoughts, words, and actions match. When don't they match? Do your thoughts, words, and actions line up with your beliefs and values? Where do you need an integrity makeover? Pick one area where you're willing to live more in integrity and outline the specific actions you will take. Acknowledge yourself every time you make the choice to live in integrity.

❧ **Chapter 15** ❧

"I'm Sorry"

Two of the most important words in the English language are *I'm sorry*. They are incredibly humbling, they allow for connection, and they support change. They are an olive branch extended to begin the healing process.

I've found that the healthiest people can say "I'm sorry" quickly and easily. It feels sincere and natural and believable. These people honor mistakes as part of life. However, many people live in either the land of over-apologizing or the land of never apologizing. We all need to strive for the land in the middle: the land of the sincere apology.

If you are an over-apologizer, then you jump at any and every chance to say, "I'm sorry." And most likely you say it more than once - probably to the point of groveling. What I want to say to you is this: "You are not to blame for all the errors of the world, who you are is not wrong, and you don't make any more mistakes than the rest of humankind." Next time you catch yourself saying "I'm sorry" more than a couple of times, take a deep breath – don't say it again, and know you've done your part to heal whatever it is that needs healing.

If you live in the land of never apologizing, then your goal is to start saying it anytime there is a mess (big or small) in any relationship. Saying "I'm sorry" means you're taking responsibility for your part in this relationship. Dr. Phil says, "We are each 100 percent responsible for our 50 percent of the relationship," and I couldn't agree more. No matter what the disagreement was, each of you had a part in it; suck it up, own your part, and apologize. Will it be humbling and hard? Maybe. Will it be worth it? Absolutely!

For the health of your relationships, it is critical to find peace with this process. It's all about taking responsibility and admitting it when things go wrong. Remember, we all make mistakes. So don't play "saint," thinking you never screw up, or "sinner," thinking everything is your fault. Instead, apologize for your piece of the mess and be willing to accept the apology from the other person for their piece.

Your Action Step: Reflect on a recent event where you had been embarrassed about your behavior, or on a situation that left a loved one sad or hurt. Find the courage to tell them "I'm sorry." Make it sincere and truthful, and see what unfolds.

Chapter 16

Forgiveness

"Forgiveness is releasing the hope that the past will change. Refusing to forgive is like drinking poison and hoping the other person will die."

~Dr. Roger Teel

In my years of working with individuals and couples, forgiveness is a consistent place where people struggle. People often believe forgiveness means "I accept the situation." For others, it means "I must allow this person back into my life." For others still, it means "If I've really forgiven this person, then I wouldn't remember the painful event anymore."

Truly, the meat of forgiveness centers around the gentle knowledge that the situation happened, and having the courage and willingness to clean up your end of the mess. It takes strength and fortitude to not let it run your life anymore. Forgiveness doesn't mean that your mind is erased of the experience, but rather that your soul has grown beyond the experience.

Forgiveness is the amazing process of stepping out of "victim consciousness" and into "grace consciousness." This is the place where you're beginning to find peace around whatever happened and to become open to healing the wounds. Which relationships in your life, including your relationship with yourself, need a little bit more grace?

I have two specific resources for my Forgiveness chapter that have supported me and my clients on our journeys:

- One is a book called *Radical Forgiveness* by Colin Tipping. This book has a bit of a different twist on forgiveness, in that it is completely an internal process and whatever happened, happened so you could grow and be, or become, the person you are meant to be. It will stretch you, but it's very effective.

- The other forgiveness practice I use regularly is the Ho'oponopono prayer. Get a picture of the person involved or call up an image of them in your mind and recite the following four statements: "_____, I love you. I'm sorry. Please forgive me. Thank you." It will irritate your logical mind, especially if you feel the other person is to blame, but it's a spiritual process that works (especially if you don't question it but instead just do it for a week or more).

Remember, forgiveness is a process and a journey that cannot be rushed; nor can it be ignored if you want your relationships to flourish.

Your Action Step: Who or what needs forgiveness in your life? Either do one of the above forgiveness practices, use another resource, or write a letter (long and detailed) to this other person and then, instead of giving it to them, burn it as a commitment to truly letting it go. Remember to include yourself in forgiveness work; for you are human and you will make mistakes, but you shouldn't let those mistakes run your life.

✌ Chapter 17 ✍

Laugh, Laugh, Laugh

When it comes right down to it, people are quirky, funky, and sometimes just odd. We do the silliest things. We make some really stupid mistakes. We say some of the oddest things, act totally weird sometimes, and can be just plain goofy. OH WELL!

Isn't that what makes this journey so much fun? We can make it fun if we're willing to laugh at how completely off we can be sometimes. We have to learn to find the humor in the hard moments – maybe not right in the moment (that could actually make things worse), but hopefully we can laugh about it later.

In our home, I'm the barometer for how things are going. When things are off, out of balance, or out of sync, I'm the first to feel it. Sometimes it triggers me and I get mad. When I'm mad, I don't yell or hit; I get quiet. The whole family knows I'm mad and that something is brewing. Eventually, I'll find an opening and share what's going on. Generally, we talk through the issue, we handle the emotions, and whenever possible we find a solution. And then we laugh – we laugh long and hard. Once I'm cooled down enough to talk and we've worked through the heart of the matter, then I'm completely willing to look at how silly I've been acting and call myself on it. The family appreciates that I can see my own shortcomings, I appreciate that they don't laugh at me before we have talked, and we all appreciate a good laugh after the intensity of a disagreement.

Karen Kolberg said it best: "Laughter is a softening influence which prevents hardening of one's heart." Laughter is good for the soul, good for the body, and good for your relationships. So where do you need to laugh more? Where can you lighten up? Where do you need to stop taking life and yourself so seriously? Find these spots and make a point to laugh about your humanness – we are, after all, a rather quirky species.

Your Action Step: Without making yourself wrong, find three opportunities to laugh at yourself and with others this week. Enjoy the feelings and the added stress-reducing benefits that laughter brings.

Chapter 18

"You Have Lettuce in Your Teeth"

Originally this seemed like an odd topic to have in this book and yet, as I wrote about laughter in the previous chapter, it felt fitting to address a topic we've all faced regularly. You know the situation – we've all been there as a witness and as the guilty party – you notice something that could potentially be embarrassing for you to tell another person or that could be embarrassing for that person if they find out about it later. Common examples are: lettuce in their teeth, a stain on their tie, toilet paper stuck to their shoe, a booger showing, hair sticking straight up, their fly is unzipped, their shirt is buttoned incorrectly, way too much perfume or cologne, etc.

What do you do about it – do you tell them or not? This is a topic that stirs up a comment from everyone, because we've all been there. Most people vote for "TELL ME! Be as discreet as possible but PLEASE tell me." Now, for some people, it's really easy to say, "Psst, you have lettuce in your teeth." Others are afraid they might embarrass the other person, so they don't say anything. But the problem is it will be more embarrassing for the person with lettuce in their teeth if they go through an entire day like this and no one says anything.

My general philosophy is, if this potentially embarrassing situation can be changed, then find a discreet way to tell the person. Lettuce in the teeth – tell them. Toilet paper stuck to their shoe – tell them. Stain on the tie – tell them if they have another tie, don't tell them if there is no solution. You get the idea, and here's another filter to use – *would I want to know?* I am personally mortified at the thought of having a booger showing – it makes me wince just thinking about it! This one can be especially hard to say to someone, "Psst, Mary, you have a booger showing." Truly, it feels embarrassing to even write – but please, on the more delicate items like this one, if you are close enough to the person, tell them. They will thank you and may even repay the favor.

Your Action Step: The next time you are faced with the dilemma, "Should I say something or just mind my own business?" ask yourself, "Would I want to know?" and then act upon your response.

⧼ Chapter 19 ⧽

Gratitude – The Great Relationship Saver

Many of us have a tendency, when we have been in a relationship for a while, to find annoying little things to nitpick on: the dishes aren't done, there are clothes on the floor, he channel-surfs, or she talks too much. These little things chip away at the foundation of a relationship, almost like termites on a wood deck. If not dealt with, these little things can be the demise of what was once a beautiful relationship.

Fortunately, tools like gratitude are a sure-fire way to get rid of relationship termites quickly and easily. The catch for some is saving gratitudes until something big comes along. My theory is to express gratitude as often as possible during the day and to use it not just with the partner who's annoying you or the friend who's getting on your nerves, but to use it everywhere – live in an atmosphere of gratitude and be verbal about it.

Gratitude can be formal, such as "I'm grateful for..." or it can be simple, such as "Thank you." Gratitude journals are an excellent way to reflect on the many blessings in your life and, when written on a regular basis, have a profound effect on your perspective. Saying "Thank you" is a simple way to share your feelings of gratitude with the world. Consider thanking your spouse for dinner, for bringing home a paycheck, for taking out the trash, for trimming the bushes, or for cleaning up after the cat. How about thanking your kids for following curfew rules, for getting their homework done, or for helping without a big fight? Consider thanking a coworker for their idea on the project, making a fresh pot of coffee, or restocking the paper in the copy machine. It really is so simple to bring an air of gratitude to everyday life. It also serves to remind the people in your life that they are valued, appreciated, and loved.

Your Action Step: Challenge yourself to say a sincere "thank you" at least 25 times today. Notice how you feel as you do this throughout the day, and also notice how people respond differently to you.

❧ Chapter 20 ❧

Life, Liberty, and the Pursuit of Happiness

O ur country was founded on the basic principles of Life, Liberty and the Pursuit of Happiness, so let's take a moment and apply them to our relationships.

Life is a continually unfolding journey. Sometimes it's easy, but sometimes it pushes us way outside of our comfort zone. The same can be said for relationships. At times, relationships are the anchor and support for our journey through life; at other times they are the catalyst that pushes us to be more of the person we came here to be. Practice not judging any moment in life as good or bad, but rather flow with it as part of what is molding and shaping you into the person you came here to be.

Liberty is the freedom to choose how you will respond and react to all that life presents and to your ever-evolving relationships. Imagine being free to *choose* new ways to respond to your teenagers, free to *choose* how you will respond to a demanding boss, and free to *choose* how you will love and be loved. Readily embracing and embodying freedom means asking yourself, *"Am I showing up as the person I want to be in this situation and in this relationship?"*

And then we land on our ultimate and life long quest: **the Pursuit of Happiness.** It is common in relationships to believe your happiness rests in someone else's hands or to delay your happiness until the right person shows up, the kids grow up, or you win the lottery. Yet, when remembering that life is continually unfolding and we are free to choose, we settle into knowing that our happiness is up to us – right here and right now. Today, we get to choose to be happy, we get to embrace what and who is in our life with gusto, and we get to see how our connections will be enriched as we do so.

Your Action Step: Come up with five things that make you happy (taking a walk and feeling the sun on your face, a bubble bath, solving a problem, an intense workout, cooking your favorite meal, singing, stargazing, laughing). Now commit to doing one of these things every day. As you do them, notice how alive you feel and how, in those moments, you are completely free to be you.

Chapter 21

From Knowledge to Action

A wise mentor once told me: *"It's not how much you know that makes healthy relationships; it's how much you put that knowledge into action."*

This mentor couldn't have been more right. Reading a book, attending a workshop, and seeking professional help are all incredibly valuable tools and a vital part of any personal growth path. And they will make absolutely no difference in your day-to-day life or your relationships unless you practice what you have heard, read, or learned on a regular basis.

Life is our classroom. Daily interactions are the times to show up as the person you have been learning to become. Imagine how your days would be different if you came to the breakfast table, the board room, or the grocery store using the new ideas you just read about. What if you practiced communicating clearly and without judgment? What if today you found a way to express greater kindness, patience, compassion, acceptance, and love to everyone you meet? As you put these skills to work in your relationships, just know there will be times when it's easy and just seems to flow, and there will be times when it feels like nothing is working – it's okay, that's actually part of the journey of learning something new. Don't give up; instead, make a new commitment to keep at it until you find your way.

It is an exciting proposition to think of what's possible when you really live all you've been taught. *Your life will change because you change.* Give it all you've got and allow yourself the gift of richer, deeper, more loving relationships.

Your Action Step: Don't wait another minute. Pick something that will bring greater fulfillment to any relationship and practice it right now.

May your days ahead be filled with more satisfying connections and deeper love because you had the wisdom and the courage to grow through your experiences.

~Namasté

Section 2

Relationship Wisdom for Couples

A happy union is not one of perfect partners,
but the triumph of love over imperfections.
~Author Unknown

Coming together is a beginning; keeping together is progress;
working together is success.
~Henry Ford

Love is a choice you make moment to moment.
~Barbara DeAngelis

∝ Chapter 22 ೯

You, Me, and Us

There are three energies in your relationship – you, me, and us. All three need time and energy, love and attention, patience and kindness, compassion and understanding, acceptance and trust. It is vital to the health of your partnership that all three energies are fed consistently with whatever will most support them.

I'm a person who needs a lot of alone time. That's how I replenish my soul and am ready for whatever comes my way. Greg, on the other hand, needs more people time. This was never an issue until Greg changed careers and started working from our home. Previously, I would use the time Greg was at work to fill my alone time needs. I had consistent days to myself (even though I was working and taking care of the kids) to do the things I needed to do to be a better person. Greg, for many years, had his job teaching to connect with a wide variety of other people and also felt satisfied. Once Greg changed careers and was working at home, he began to miss the connections he'd had with coworkers and students, and he turned to me to fill that void. For me, having Greg working from home meant that most of the time I used to spend taking care of my needs was gone. It was an incredibly hard transition for us and we still have to make regular adjustments.

My reason for sharing this story is that neither one of us gets to have it only our way. I need to come out of my cave and be available for Greg. Greg needs to find new ways to connect with others and give me some alone time. And we both need to consciously choose to spend time that is devoted solely to our partnership and nothing else.

Find ways to meet your personal needs. Find ways to support your partner in meeting their needs. Then put focused, conscious energy into meeting the needs of your partnership. You will enjoy the balance this brings – you, me, and us – valuing all three.

Your Action Step: Create a list of things that you enjoy doing which really satisfy your soul. Then create a second list of things that nurture the relationship and your connection. Together with your partner, talk about what each of you are going to do for yourselves as individuals and what you are going to do together to build on the "us."

Chapter 23

The Reality of a Life Partnership

This tip is not meant to be the voice of doom and gloom, but rather to assure you that your partnership is okay even when it feels difficult. The truth is that sustaining any long term relationship takes work - hard work. Sure, the idea of "happily ever after" sounds nice, but that's not reality. In fact, many people don't even think beyond the wedding. They really have no concept of what it's going to be like living with the same person day in and day out.

Rest assured that just because your relationship feels like hard work doesn't mean you married the wrong person. You most likely didn't. The person you fell in love with and married is still there. It's just important to emphasize that, as daily life picks up, the newness of the relationship wears off, the kids are born, clothes don't get folded, a job is lost, a new career launched, sad and sometimes tragic losses occur – basically, as life goes on, you will need to work on your relationship to keep it alive and healthy. So lean into this and accept it. Don't dismiss your relationship because it needs some tender loving care; everything in life worth having deserves consistent mindful work.

Also keep in mind that your relationship will ebb and flow. There will be times of great connection and times of distance. Just be mindful that, in times of distance, one of you will need to find a way to reconnect, lest you drift completely apart. That's where the work comes in. Think of your relationship like a river

– always flowing and changing. Many times you flow in the river like two streams that have merged into one; things are working well, you both feel connected to common goals and to each other. Then you encounter a big boulder in that river – the two of you part to go around it – now what? Will you let this separation in your relationship be permanent or will you work to find a way to reconnect? The tips in this book can serve as reminders and teachers of ways to reconnect to each other.

Living your relationship with the conscious awareness that there will be times of distance, times of feeling less connected and loving, and times of more individualization allows you to be ready and willing to do the work to keep your relationship alive. Our relationship has certainly had times of hard work, times of distance, times of boredom – but when I look back on the journey we've traveled, trusting that Greg is in it with me for the long haul, I know I'm willing to do whatever it takes to bring us back together when we encounter a boulder.

Your Action Step: If you are feeling solidly connected to your partner right now, spend time talking about how you got to this place. Reflecting helps to anchor what you did well. If you are feeling disconnected or like this is just too hard, then do two things: first, make a date to go play. No serious talk for those few hours, just find a way to play and enjoy each other's company. Second, set up another time to talk about what you can each do to build your relationship connection and remind each other that the hard work is worth it because your relationship is worth it.

Chapter 24

Timing Is Everything

E very relationship is going to have tough topics to address. These can range from finances to in-laws, sex to parenting, nights with friends to time alone. Most of these will surface and then resurface until eventually an agreement is reached.

You will have greater success solving these issues if you practice timing your discussions. This is where prefacing (see Chapter 9) comes in really handy. "Honey we need to talk about our finances. When would you like to schedule a couple of hours to do this?"

To blast your partner when your emotions are running high will practically guarantee a fight and hurt feelings. If you hit your partner with a serious topic when they have just come home from work, most likely you are not going to have their full attention and focus. To try and talk about sex with the kids in the room – nope, that's just not going to support the discussion. If you must say something at these inappropriate times, use a prefacing statement to get the ball rolling and then wait until you are both ready, willing, and emotionally present to launch into these important discussions.

On the upside, when you appropriately time your big discussions, your actions are saying, "I respect you enough to wait until you are ready to talk and I respect myself enough to set up our discussions for a better chance of success."

Your Action Step: Consider the times in your relationship where either you or your partner had bad timing when addressing an important issue. Now consider how timing things better might have supported your relationship. How can you practice using this skill this week?

Chapter 25

"I Am Not a Home Improvement Project!"

I want to believe that who I am is good enough for Greg. Greg wants to believe that he's good enough for me. So as soon as one of us starts making the other one our "personal home improvement project," that "good enough" feeling goes flying out the window. I'm not saying each of us doesn't have room to change, evolve, grow, and become a better person – after all, we are never finished products – but I am saying that how you address things with your partner is huge.

Consider this example: being the loving wife/partner you are, you thought: "Once we get married, I'll get him a new wardrobe." While this seems like a nice gesture, did you ask him what he wanted? Did you ask him if he likes the way he dresses and if it works for him professionally? Did he ask for your guidance in this area? If all the answers are <u>no,</u> then you are treading in the "home improvement" area and my comment is: "Please stop until you talk to him and see what he wants."

My intention here is not to pick on the wives, because this issue (like all of them in this book) is not gender-specific. I have known just as many guys who want to "fix" their women without their permission. Think of the guy who signs up his wife or partner for a gym membership without discussing it with her – same thing. She has become his "home improvement project."

Remember, if you do these seemingly nice gestures without discussing them first, the message is clear: "Who you are right now is not what I want." I know that most of the time when people do these things, they really are doing it out of the goodness in their heart and wanting to improve the quality of your life. So, let's hold onto that truth while also asking that your partner talk to you before taking on any personal changes for you, and then you do the same for him or her.

Your Action Step: In what area would you like your partner to change? Write it down and then have a gentle loving discussion with him or her to see if that's something your partner wants to change, if he or she would appreciate your support, and how you can do it together.

❧ Chapter 26 ❧

Give Each Other Time to Process

I'm a person who wants to handle an issue immediately. Greg, on the other hand, needs a bit of time to pull his thoughts together and be ready to talk and listen. This was agonizing in the beginning of our relationship. Something would happen and I'd start pecking (asking questions, probing; doing anything to draw him out) and his reaction would be to go further and further into himself. Because of this escalated behavior on both our parts, the wounds of the disagreement were much bigger and it took us longer to heal.

During premarital counseling, we brought this difference to our minister. She acknowledged our desire to work through the problem, and then she helped us set parameters around how to handle disagreements better. Greg owned up to the fact that he's just not ready to talk right after something happens. He needs a good night's sleep and a shower, and then he'll talk. My fear said, "If I give him this space then we'll never talk about it." So, he agreed that after those two things he'd come to me and say he was ready to talk. We practiced this skill – he built trust that I would give him space to process and I built trust that he would initiate the discussion. It has made our disagreements so much more civil. We are both more willing to listen to each other and, through the trust that has been built, we are both at peace knowing we're going work through the issue.

So what kind of parameters does your partnership need – an

hour, half a day, a good night's sleep? It could also be situational – sometimes Greg only needs an hour and sometimes he needs several days before he can talk. Agree on the parameters for your relationship and then follow them when disagreements or fights arise. It's such a respectful way to say to your partner, "I love you enough to give you what you need because I'm also getting what I need."

The added bonus – allowing time to process (usually 24 to 48 hours) – also engages more of your rational mind so when you do talk (and listen), there is a greater probability that you'll be able to reach a solution or compromise. And maybe you'll even be able to laugh about what just unfolded.

Your Action Step: Set up a time – when you are feeling connected and unemotional – to talk to your partner about your "disagreement processing time." Listen to each other's point of view with an open mind and a willingness to collaborate. Then come up with an agreement as to how processing time will look in your relationship. Not only verbally come up with a plan, but also write it out. Remember, when we're upset, our skills tend to fade; having your plan in writing will remind each of you what you've agreed to.

Chapter 27

Sex Does Matter

You want to see couples start squirming? Ask them how their sex life is, and tell them to be honest. No fair asking newlyweds – sex is hot when you're fresh in the relationship. It's easy, everybody's willing, you have loads of energy for it, you're willing to do it almost anywhere – you get the picture.

For more established couples, couples with kids, or couples where the infatuation is clearly worn off, sex can begin to wane. So many things have the potential to interfere with a couple's sex life: kids, work, sleep patterns, sex drive, age, financial challenges, job changes, hormones, medication, and the busyness of life.

Sex is a valuable and important part of a monogamous relationship. It builds intimacy, provides for physical and emotional connection, and releases stress. So while there are great books on the topic and professionals who specialize in it, my words of wisdom here are "Be willing to talk about it." And keep talking about it until you find something that works for both of you. Then revisit the topic whenever there seem to be changes in your sex life.

One more vital piece of advice: don't compare your sex life to anyone else's. Every partnership is different and the two people in the partnership are different; your sex life will be different, too. Comparing only leads to heartache and feelings of inadequacy. Find what's right for you and your partner and then nourish it.

Your Action Step: Find a quiet space, free from distraction, and ask your partner to share what's working in your sex life and what needs a bit of tweaking. Then, you do the same thing – share what's working and what needs tweaking. Look for ways that both of you can be more satisfied. A reminder to please be gentle with the tweaking pieces, as this can be a very sensitive subject, and try to leave your ego out of it. Remember, this is about having a better sex life and both of you may need to change a few things.

Chapter 28

Take Responsibility for Your Part

If your relationship is working, you get half the credit. If your relationship isn't working, you are half responsible. Learn to own up to this fact; stop blaming your partner when things go wrong and do your part to clean it up.

I know this is not the easiest step. Blaming comes fast and furious when things get heated. We can always see what our partner is doing to contribute to this mess, but we can't always see what we've done wrong ourselves.

Finances are a frequent source of contention for many couples. The spender blames the saver for not being able to live life to the fullest, or for being cheap. The saver blames the spender for spending frivolously or not being focused on long term goals. This is an easy area to blame the other person for what's not working. Imagine taking responsibility for your part of the mess. Perhaps the spender would be willing to consider where they could cut back or how they could learn to spend a little less. An even more valuable process might be looking at the need to spend and where that comes from. The saver could listen to the spender and perhaps create a more realistic budget – one that meets both the need to save and the need to live for today. The saver would also be served by looking at any fears around "not having enough" – where did that come from and is it true today? Through personal reflection and personal responsibility, this couple has a chance to find common financial goals and work together to achieve them.

Take time whenever the pot is stirred up – or if things are simply not as good as you'd like them to be – and ask: "How did I contribute to this situation?" With practice, you will begin to see your patterns, your process, and your shortcomings, and then you can make positive changes. You see, we really can't change another human being – we can only make suggestions for ways they could live differently or perhaps better. They are the ones who must decide to change, and ultimately do it for themselves and not you. You have the opportunity to do the same – you get to decide to change and evolve right along with the relationship. The best way to do this is to take responsibility for your 50 percent of the relationship.

Your Action Step: Take a quick inventory of the current state of your relationship and ask, "What are three things I did or didn't do that got us to this place?" Then share your answer with your partner, ask him or her to answer the same question, and create a plan that works towards a solution.

Chapter 29

"I Love You, but I'm Not in Love with You Anymore!"

We are all familiar with this phrase, having either experienced it ourselves or having heard it in movies. It's not all that uncommon, and it can serve as a very generic excuse to end a relationship. For me, when I hear it, my first reaction is to roll my eyes and groan. It seems like a big cop-out. What is this person really saying? What are they afraid to say? What's really happening?

Here is what I hear when someone says this:

- "I love you, but I'm bored."
- "I love you, but I don't want to work this hard."
- "I love you, but I'm not feeling the chemical high of infatuation so I have to leave."
- "I love you, but you've changed and it's too hard to talk about."
- "I love you, but the grass is greener elsewhere and I want to play over there."

Committed relationships take consistent loving work. No one can get married and then hope the marriage will manage itself; it doesn't work like that. Think of your love like a fire – when you first build it, you make it big like a bonfire. You put your creativity into it, your energy, your enthusiasm – you invest in the fire to make it work. And then if you want that fire to continue, you keep adding fuel or the fire dies. The same thing is true in a committed relationship – you must keep investing in it in order to keep that loving feeling. It absolutely will not happen on its own.

Now, I do know that sometimes relationships end. Sadly, it does happen. People sometimes do grow apart and destructive things happen that can't be repaired. But please, before you go the route of ending your relationship, invest some time, energy, and hard work to see if you can rekindle the fire. You've built a life with this person; do what you can to remember why you chose that route.

Your Action Step: Ask yourself what you can do today to add life, zest, and love to your relationship – then go do exactly that. It doesn't have to be a big production – a love note on the mirror, a golf outing, a special meal, flowers, taking a walk and holding hands, having sex – get creative and see what happens. Also consider talking to your partner about areas where the relationship is dry, boring, or unfulfilling and see what the two of you together can do to improve things.

❧ Chapter 30 ❧

Love, Acknowledge, and Appreciate

Imagine a relationship where you remember why you fell in love with your partner and they remember why they fell in love with you. Imagine verbally acknowledging your partner for the large and the small things they do to make life better, and imagine being acknowledged by your partner for what you do. Imagine expressing genuine appreciation for your partner and being appreciated in kind. Doesn't that just sound delightful?

Let me assure you – it is! This is one exercise that Greg and I use whenever we need a boost, and one I use with every couple I've ever worked with. It's the exercise I *guarantee* will have a positive impact on your relationship, especially when it is done on a regular basis.

Here's how the process works:

- Each of you grab a clean sheet of paper and write down three things you love about your partner (things that are inherently them: their laugh, their blue eyes, their craftsmanship, their kind soul, etc.). Start each sentence with: "Something I love about you is…"

- Next, write down three acknowledgments (things they did that day for their own growth, health, forward motion, etc.: working out even though they were tired, getting the project done on time and done well, having that difficult conversation with their mother, etc.). Start each sentence with: "Something I acknowledge you for is…"

- Lastly, write down three things you appreciate about your partner (things that they do to contribute to the relationship: going to work every day, taking out the trash, cleaning up after the cat, taking the car in for repairs, listening when you have a bad day, etc.). Start each sentence with: "Something I appreciate about you is…"

This exercise is a gift to your relationship. It helps you focus on the positive and reminds you why you've chosen this person as your partner. It will enrich your lives and expand your love.

Your Action Step: Do the above exercise daily for three weeks and watch what happens to your relationship. It only takes about 10 to 15 minutes to write and another 10 to 15 minutes to share. Are you ready to invest 20 to 30 minutes and get a BIG return?

Chapter 31

Support, Support, Support

Your relationship needs healthy support to thrive. Many couples don't think they need the support of others – they can handle everything themselves – or they believe their issues aren't big enough for support. Maybe they just don't feel very connected. Maybe they're embarrassed to ask for support because surely that means they're a failure. The biggest tragedy might be that they go to the wrong people for support.

Imagine being really upset with your partner and in that moment of pain and anger you think that the only option is leaving. So you go to your best friend, who's single, lonely, and sometimes a bit jealous of your marriage – do you really think this person is going to be objective and not tell you to leave? Or imagine feeling bored with your relationship and you tell a buddy who has just had an affair – don't you think this person might encourage you to do the same?

Healthy support is vital to the strength of the marriage. Maybe you're one of the lucky ones and some of the people in your life are healthy and objective – great! Many don't have that luxury and so I'm encouraging you to find another option. Perhaps there is a couples group in your church. Maybe you could find an older couple who would be willing to be your marriage mentors, or you could find another couple (or several) that have solid marriages and create a couples support group.

That's what we did. We formed a couples support group when our youngest was six months old. This group meets once a month to discuss a relationship topic. As we got closer over the years, we would also bring our personal relationship challenges to the group to get their thoughts and ideas. It has been a lifesaver on more than one occasion, and it consistently reconnects us. We have put the "how to" into a book called *Preventative Maintenance for Your Marriage: The Owner's Manual for a Couples Group.* We have grown over the years into really good friends, but we initially started with these people because they seemed to have solid marriages and were committed to making it work. Whatever route you choose, just be aware that your partnership needs support.

Your Action Step: Explore with your partner what kind of support you both feel would be best for your relationship. Then set a specific time and date that you will actually engage this support.

Section 3

Relationship Wisdom for Parents

Parenthood is just the world's most intensive course in love.
~Polly Berrien Berends

*"I have many flowers," he said. "But the Children are
the most beautiful flowers of all."*
~Oscar Wilde

*Though no one can go back and make a brand new start,
anyone can start now and make a brand new ending.*
~Author Unknown

Chapter 32

Appreciating Every Age/Stage

Kids are an amazing addition to your life, one that is entirely different than anything else you've ever experienced. They are an extension of you, but they are not you. They have needs, desires, goals, wishes, and demands; and are a general hub of boundless activity.

Each age and stage of your child's life will bring wonderful things that make your heart swell with joy, love, and pride. And each stage will bring challenges, frustration, sleepless nights, and doubts.

What I've found over the years is that the smartest thing I can do is to savor the really sweet and precious parts of each age and stage, and have memory lapses on the rest. If you dwell on the challenges, it makes parenting really hard.

When my kids were infants, having them fall asleep in my arms was the most wonderful feeling in the world – it makes me smile just to remember it. Changing dirty diapers, getting up three times a night, and not knowing why they were crying are the parts of this stage I don't miss at all.

Toddlers carry such sweet innocence and have such a delight in their eyes at anything and everything. Their unconditional love and belief that I was "Super Mom" were amazing feelings. I don't miss the energy drain of those happy-go-lucky little people.

From kindergarten through grade five, I loved watching them learn, going on field trips, beginning to have conversations, and learning to listen better. I didn't really enjoy all the school projects they needed help with or all the times they were really sick. For us, school seemed to start the process of building immunity, so my kids got everything that was going around.

Everyone says the teenage years are the hardest, but I find that they are just like all the other stages. There are good parts – the real talks, their developing skills and passions, their humor, and their growing independence – and there are challenging parts – being called on inconsistencies, fighting you when you say no, and pushing back a little harder.

Make it a point to notice the gifts – the special moments that are only shared by you and your kids. Savor them, because they really do pass quickly. And that goes for those really trying moments – they too will pass quickly.

Your Action Step: Today, pick something you love about the age or stage your kids are at and tell them about it.

❧ Chapter 33 ❧

Accepting Your Kids for Who They Are

K ids come into this world with two criteria. One is to learn and be molded into the person they are meant to be. The other is to be honored for their uniqueness and be respected for the person they are.

Yes, it is absolutely our job to teach our kids how life works from our perspective. This includes sharing our values, teaching right from wrong, showing them how to do a wide variety of household chores and projects, teaching responsibility, and teaching them the importance of being accountable for their actions. Actually, the list of things they will learn from us is much longer. As parents, a gift we offer our children is being open to teaching them and sharing the wisdom we've gleaned over the years.

Equally as vital is the need to respect who they are as individuals and not push in ways that devalue their inherent nature. Imagine children who are introverts – forcing them to be more extroverted is a waste of time, and it sends the message: "Who you are, by nature, is wrong." And what about children who have bundles of energy and natural athletic ability? Do you think they are wrong because they can't sit still, or do you find ways to expel that energy and use that talent? Consider children who are sensitive, quiet, funny, or talkative; these are qualities that make them unique individuals.

Finding the balance between something that can be taught and something that is their inherent nature can be a slippery slope, but it's definitely worth exploring. At least, keep an open mind to the fact that maybe whatever it is that you're proposing might not be a good fit for your child. All of us have witnessed parents who shame their children when they don't live up to the parents' expectations – let's do our best to not be one of those parents. Remember, it can be tough as a parent to know when your kids need a bit of a push and when to refrain from pushing because the result is truly not who they are. So go easy on yourself if you've messed up in this area – I know we have. But little by little, their true nature does emerge. Their strengths begin to shine and so do the areas where your encouragement will be needed. Trust your instincts to know when to push and when to allow something to be dropped completely.

Your Action Step: Today, take note of the characteristics that are inherent and unique in each of your children. Appreciate them for these special qualities and ask yourself (and them) how else you can nurture these characteristics.

Chapter 34

Talk, Talk, Talk

Talk, talk, talk to your kids. Believe it or not, they want to hear what you have to say – even if they act like they aren't listening.

Think of talking to your kids in two ways: offering sound bites here and there, and occasionally having longer, deeper discussions. Sound bites can happen all day long, everyday. Those few little words spoken here and there really are heard and really do matter. Oh sure, the kids might act like they aren't listening and may not follow through (especially when the sound bites involve chores), but spend a day not talking to your kids and see how they respond. Most likely they'll be following you around wanting to know what's going on. So talk to them: ask about their day, tell them about yours, share an interesting story you heard, leave comics on their chair, find out what their friends are up to. As you talk more to them, apply this same idea and listen for the sound bites coming back to you – I have learned amazing things about my kids in those passing words that are thrown in my direction. Honestly, I think they throw them out to see if I'm really listening to them.

The longer, deeper discussions could be saved for family meetings, when something is really important and needs more than a sound bite (i.e., talking about sex, drugs, school challenges, etc.) or if they've messed up and you are talking through what happened and why. It is critical in longer discussions to be aware of moments when your kids' eyes glaze over and they check out. This often occurs because they feel they are being talked at, not talked to. When this happens, it's time to either table the discussion until later, find a way to bring them more fully into the discussion by asking for their thoughts about what you're saying, or shift the conversation for a moment or two to someone or something else. It doesn't do anyone any good to keep going if the listener has checked out – in fact, in our house, this is when tempers begin to flare for both the parents ("they're not listening") and the kids ("they're lecturing me and I can't hear anymore").

Please don't clam up. Don't think your kids don't care (they do), and don't get quiet just because Junior is acting like he's not listening. Keep your relationship alive and active by talking to your kids.

Your Action Step: Make a commitment to do one of the following:

- Throw out a few sound bites and see what happens.
- Have a family meeting with a clear agenda and a set time.
- Take your kids out for ice cream and have three powerful questions ready for them. Examples might be: What have you done recently that you're proud of? If you could do anything, big or small, this weekend, what would it be? Who is your best friend and what makes them a best friend to you?

∾ Chapter 35 ∾

And Listen Too!

The last chapter was all about talking, and most likely your thoughts are starting to flow around "How can I talk to my kids more?" The flip side of this process is that you also need to listen more.

If you ask them about their day, listen for the answer – and really care about what they have to say. If you ask them about their friends – again, really listen for an answer – don't try to solve any issues. Sometimes kids don't want to talk to us because we automatically want to problem-solve. Just like us, they don't always want a solution; they just want to share. If you think they want help solving anything, then ask them.

Not too long ago, our daughter was having an issue with a friend. I practiced listening – a lot. I was listening for sadness in her voice, listening for any new information that she might want to share, and listening for how she was dealing with all of it. It wasn't easy; I really wanted to jump in and tell her how to fix it. I tried a few times, and her reaction was to clam up. So I backed off and did my best to just listen. This went on for several weeks before she was willing to hear my thoughts and ideas. Once she was open to hearing what I had to say, I offered it to her in a sound bite; nothing long and drawn out, just enough to help her see that there were other ways to handle the issue.

This, like so many other conversations we've had with the kids, is all about looking for the crack in the door (the possible opening) and seizing the opportunity to connect. But be careful that your seizing the opportunity doesn't come across like a steam roller and you end up doing all the talking. Remember, listening is respectful and vital for ANY relationship, so practice it with your kids.

Your Action Step: Stop what you're doing for just a few minutes today, and listen — really listen — to your kids. Then ponder what you learned.

Chapter 36

Parenting is a Team Sport

Kids, by their very nature, force us out of our comfort zone every single day. To be good or even great parents, you must be willing to jump in with both feet and do the things that don't feel easy, familiar, or natural.

If you are a single parent, you are forced into all the parenting and household roles by default; and I sincerely hope that you find support along the way. Parenting is hard enough with two people, so to those of you who have to or choose to go it alone, my hat is off to you with great respect. Again, I stress, find support wherever and whenever you can. Please don't be too proud to ask – it really does take a village to raise healthy kids.

For the two-parent families, it's easy to get pigeonholed into "that's your job" and "this is my job" with rigidly defined boundaries. Remember, this is not the 1950s; things are very different now, and parenting works best when it's hands-on for both of you. So where in your mind do you think, "That's his job" or "That's her job"? Those are the situations I want you to question and talk about. Yes, it's good to have someone who is basically in charge, but that doesn't mean the other person shouldn't contribute in these areas.

Perhaps you are the primary breadwinner and you think that's all you have to do. Sadly, let me pop that bubble. Your role as primary breadwinner is highly valued in the family, and necessary. However, that does not excuse you from changing a diaper, driving the car pool, helping with homework, or generally being an active parent. Both parents need to be involved in all aspects of their kids' lives – especially if they want solid lasting relationships with their kids. (Think of people you know who don't have much of a relationship with their father because all he did was work; it's very sad for everyone that he missed out on so much.) Remember, being involved doesn't mean that you are both driving the car pool; it means that you talk it out and support each other. Pick things each of you can do. I often helped with the school parties, while Greg took charge of the orthodontist appointments.

Parenting is a journey that can divide a couple; being an active and involved parent is one way to support teamwork during these chaotic, busy, and sometimes challenging years. You'll feel like you're really in it together and that will pay off down the road.

Your Action Step: Evaluate where you are a bit too hands-off as a parent, and talk to your partner about where you could contribute more.

✑ Chapter 37 ✑

Down Time? What the Heck is That?

"There is more to life than increasing its speed."
~Mahatma Gandhi

With the upsurge of technology, things that used to take years are at our fingertips in an instant. And with that comes the desire to do it all. We not only pack our schedules, we pack our kids' schedules with all kinds of activities that we think will bring happiness and create well-rounded adults. We want them to be physically active, to have brain stimulation, and to socialize. We encourage them to grow through a large variety of different experiences and to explore far and wide. There is nothing wrong with any of this, until we get to the point that our eight-year-old has a Day-Timer to keep his schedule straight; or our teenager is doing homework at 11 p.m. because he or she had a volleyball game, a homecoming meeting, a viola lesson, and two hours of service work at church. Yikes!

Ok, so I am a realist; I do know that sometimes you can't avoid days like the one I mentioned above, but my hope is that they are the exception, not the rule in your house. As odd as it may sound, we consciously underschedule our kids' activities rather than overschedule them. And I'm fully aware that we may be in the minority with this topic. We have simply not been willing to run ourselves or our kids ragged by overscheduling their extra curricular activities.

The upside to more modest scheduling is that all of us have unstructured down time. Our society seems to run on stress, and that's one thing we'd rather not encourage and pass along. Down time has been our solution. Down time in our house has been used for TV and video games. Many might say that's a waste of time. And when it's in excess, it is a waste of time, so that's something to be mindful of. Other uses of down time have included going on walks, playing cards and board games, having unrushed conversations, playing baseball in the yard, reading a good book, setting up skateboarding ramps in the street, learning to bake, and – the family favorite – rescuing stray pets. We've had spontaneous fun and this has supported more of a stress-free environment. I don't know if you need that, but I certainly do, and I want to teach my kids how to savor unstructured time.

Your Action Step: Do an honest evaluation of your schedules, and if it feels too overscheduled, consider making an adjustment (start small and build into your ideal schedule). Or next time you find a bit of unstructured, unscheduled time, don't fight it; instead, find a way to enjoy it completely and with wild abandon.

❧ Chapter 38 ❧

Join Them in Their World

Kids are people too and deserve respect just like the rest of us. From infancy to young adulthood, be willing to join them in their world.

Think about toddlers and how much fun they have creating things, playing in the dirt, dancing – they are active beings eager for your attention. So be willing to go there with them. Play in the mud, do a craft with them, or turn on the music and dance. Greg used to have rubber duck races in the street after a big rain storm. For some of you, cutting loose with your toddler will completely take you out of your comfort zone; do it anyway, as it will create some of the best memories you will ever have.

As they grow, joining them in their world takes many different twists. School years can mean volunteering in the classroom, going on field trips, coaching their soccer team, or being the Girl Scout or Boy Scout leader. Do anything that shows your kids that you value what they are doing. We adults can so easily get swept up in the day-to-day minutiae – work, house chores, managing the bills, continuing to feed our own hobbies – that we believe we don't have time to join them in their world. We truly must make time – it forges bonds and builds self-esteem in them when they know they matter enough for us to put aside our own agenda and do child-centered activities.

The kids growing up today are technologically savvy. Technology is in their world to stay, and it does absolutely no good to ignore it or fight against it. So it's equally as important to join them in this world. If they like video games, then play video games with them sometimes. Trust me, they won't care if you stink at it; in fact, it makes it even more fun for them to have something they are better at than Mom or Dad. You don't have to become great at it, just take an interest.

We were a "no cell phone" family until our kids were in the later years of middle school. By then, most of their friends had phones and we chose not to fight it any longer. Honestly, it's been one of the best things I've ever surrendered to. My kids are completely willing to text me as a way to keep in touch. I certainly know more about where my kids are and what they're doing than my parents ever did.

Consider where you can join your kids in their world and go for it. Remember, I'm not suggesting you need to play video games all day on Saturday with Junior; even a half hour will show respect and interest. And have fun! You never know what new adventures are out there for you to enjoy.

Your Action Step: Find something from your kids' world that you can join them in today – and remember to laugh a lot; especially, be willing to laugh at yourself.

✌ Chapter 39 ✌

Consequences vs. Punishment

My son, in the throes of his teenage years, complimented Greg and me one day on the fact that, when he screws up, we instill consequences and not punishment. I thought that was incredibly insightful for a 14-year-old and started pondering, "What really is the difference between them?"

Consequences, or "cause and effect," should fit the infraction. If they mess up with friends, then they need time away from their friends. If their grades fall, then take the video games away so they can focus more on school work. If they mouth off to us, then they need to go in their room, away from us, until they can apologize and tell us why it wasn't okay to talk like that. If they are inappropriate with another adult, then they go (escorted by us) to that adult, apologize, and see what they can do to make it right. Whatever the crime, the consequence is directly related – it's not always easy to find the direct correlation, but taking the time to find a way to tie it in makes sense to the kid.

Punishment, on the other hand, has a harshness to it - an out-of-control, "my parents lost it" feeling. This could range from violent yelling and cussing at your child to abusive physical contact to unreasonable jobs and chores. The biggest thing is that punishment feels mean – and kids know it. You are lashing out inappropriately and this is not a fun place for anyone to be.

Kids are really smart and are trying their hardest to figure out how the world works. Having the consequences fit the infraction helps your kids put things in place for later in life, and this is one big way to build trust with them. It sends the message that you are going to be fair and you aren't going to blow things out of proportion. Then if something big does come along, your child knows that you'll be rational and work through it; leaving them with the sense that everything is going to be OK.

Your Action Step: Next time one of your kids makes a mistake, specifically look for a consequence that is directly related to what they did. Take note of how it changes the family dynamic.

Chapter 40

The High-Low Game

We learned about the High-Low game from a movie, *The Story of Us*. Since I'm all for finding ways to get our kids to talk, this has become one of our favorites and it hasn't gone out of style as they have grown. We have often played High-Low around the dinner table, but have also been known to use it at other times too – on a plane returning from vacation, in the car after a family event, or when their friends are over as a way to get to know them. It's an inviting way for each person to share about their day or their experience. Simply put, each person takes a turn and tells the high point of their day or experience and the low point of their day or experience. It's good to ask a few follow-up questions, but be mindful that no one gets too long-winded; you want to make sure each person has a chance to share.

Often, through sound bites that occur naturally throughout the day, we will hear about either the high or the low of their day, but consciously doing this activity gives us both sides of the equation. So, even if they've had a bad day and you've already heard about it, now you get a chance to hear what was good about their day. And this will give your kids the skill of knowing that even when they've have a bad day, there was still something good about it.

The added bonus with the High-Low game is that it not only gives us quick information about what's happening with our kids, but it also gives our kids quick information about what's happening with us. Kids need to be taught to ask about their parents' day. This game serves as a great way to remind them that Mom and Dad are people too, and that they also have highs and lows to deal with. It really begins to teach them empathy and a greater understanding of the responsibilities of being an adult.

Your Action Step: Tonight at dinner, use the High-Low game – even with toddlers, and even if friends are over – and find out what's happening in their world. Be willing to share a bit of what's happening in your world. (Just a quick side note: this can be a great conversation starter for couples too – maybe on a date or when the house is quiet and it's just the two of you.)

ᕔ Chapter 41 ᕗ

Potpourri for Parents

Here are a few reminders that will also serve your parenting journey:

- Affection: Healthy, respectful affection can be one of the greatest gifts that kids bring to your household. If you are a person who enjoys hugs, then hug your kids a lot. If you are not particularly affectionate yourself, then just see if you can find a few little moments here and there where you could offer a hug, a pat on the shoulder, or a gentle touch. Healthy affection offers your kids an unspoken measure of reassurance, comfort, and unconditional love.

- Chores: Kids are not your personal slaves, and yet they are members of the household and will need to participate in keeping things running. It can be really hard to know when you're asking too much of them and when you're asking too little. This is especially true since any work issue will almost always brings up a bit of grumbling. The most important thing is be realistic and question yourself every now and then to see if you're expecting too much or too little involvement from your children. While being involved in household work can create strong ethics, it can also build resentment. As parents, we can easily forget that kids need time to be kids.

- Find common ground: Seek out ways that you and your kids are alike; some of them may completely surprise you. When your kids are little, you have the advantage of introducing them to the things you like and seeing if they catch on. I love to bake, so I had Amber in the kitchen with me a lot. She is now an avid baker and has even won a few contests. As they grow up, others will expose them to new things and common ground could emerge from that. Tyler took a class in middle school that was all about rock music. He came home and played one of his new favorite songs for us – Stairway to Heaven by Led Zeppelin. We surprised Tyler by not only knowing the song but having fond memories of where it showed up in our past. Gratefully, we have since found many more songs that appeal to all three of us. We are often taught to "seek common ground" when it comes to diversity issues on our planet, so let's do that with our kids as well.

Your Action Step: Think about the above concepts and consider where you could do better. Then ask your kids their opinion on the above and have an open dialogue regarding the changes you want to make.

Section 4

Relationship Wisdom for Singles

The greatest discovery of my generation is that a human being can alter his life by altering his attitudes.
~William James

When we cannot bear to be alone,
it means we do not properly value the only companion we will have from birth to death – ourselves.
~Eda LeShan

Lots of people want to ride with you in the limo, but what you want is someone who will take the bus with you when the limo breaks down.
~Oprah Winfrey

❧ Chapter 42 ❧

Be the Best Single You Can Be

You're single – right now, anyway – so how about making it the best experience of your life? Think of it as having the ultimate relationship with yourself. Imagine waking up everyday being happy with where you are and living with gusto. Wouldn't that be the best feeling in the world?

My guess is that you have friends who seem happy with whatever stage of life they're in and you have friends who bemoan almost any stage of life they're in. It's a state of mind. Being single brings its ups and downs, its challenges and wins – just like being in a relationship does. Deciding to enjoy your reality will make being single a positive and memorable experience that you will have with you for the rest of your life.

Before Greg came into my life, I was the happiest single I'd ever been! That's because, two years earlier, I had mustered the courage to end an emotionally abusive relationship. It took me a while to pull myself together after that experience and to get on with life. But once I did, I made up my mind that I would rather be single and happy than in another abusive relationship. I started living full out. I made plans as if I might be single forever. What kind of trips did I want to take? How much money did I need to start saving for retirement? What kind of hobbies and interests did I want to participate in? I was open to a relationship, but I hadn't put my life on hold waiting for Mr. Right; in fact, I was living the life I really wanted to live and was completely at peace with being single.

So how about you – are you happy? Are you at peace with being single? Are you doing all the things you want to be doing with your life? Are you having a fantastic relationship with yourself? I say, go for it. Be the best you, right now. Not only will you love your life, but you will present an enthusiasm and joy for life that is delightful for anyone to be around.

Your Action Step: Do five things this week that shout, "I love my life!"

❧ Chapter 43 ❧

Share Your Gifts with the World

You have so many gifts that are yours and yours alone; it's time to get out there and share them with the world. As a single person, you have opportunities and discretionary time that may not be as plentiful once you're in a relationship. Why not use your talents and your passions to show the world who you really are? This is a great time to build relationships with diverse people, organizations, and causes.

This is not the time to isolate or hide; this is the time to shine. I had a single friend who was restless with her life and wanted to be married, but it wasn't happening. So she kept exploring – on a big scale – who she wanted to be, how she wanted to share her gifts with the world, and what she could do to make a difference. This friend is now in Africa teaching children, who have lost parents to AIDS, how to survive. She has created an entire organization, has raised funds to support the process, and has built two schools in the village she works with. She is an amazing example of a single person who is using her gifts to impact the world.

So what do you want to do? Is it time to go back to school? Is it time to start that business you've always wanted? Are you ready to join the Peace Corps? How about signing on as a Big Brother or Big Sister, or volunteering at an animal shelter, or taking the Red Cross training to be a disaster relief worker? Think specifically about things you enjoy that could also serve the planet in some way. It can be as large or as small as you want it to be (and as your current life style allows for). I challenge you to look beyond the fears that may come slamming up in your face – i.e., "I can't afford it," "I couldn't possibly take time off from work to do that," "I might fail," "I might succeed and everything will change." Giving in to the fears will always stop you, so start small. Start by researching different options. Then take the next step. Let it build over time – but the key is to start. The world is ready for the gifts you have to share.

Your Action Step: Right now, in this moment, own up to the fact that you have something to share with the world – yes, you! Then take one step towards sharing that gift.

❧ Chapter 44 ❧

What is Dating Anyway?

D ating is the adventure of finding new and interesting people to do things with AND dating is the process of screening potential life partners.

First of all, make the process of dating fun. It's an adventure, it gets your blood pumping, it takes you out of your comfort zone, it occupies your brain with new thoughts, and it shakes up your world. Oh sure, we've all had our bad dates, but honestly, don't those experiences also make life fun? Dating "horror stories" give us all something to talk about and unique memories to share. And those horror stories make it even more satisfying when you finally find someone you click with.

Dating is also a screening process. Take off the rose-colored glasses and really look at the person you're dating – inside and out. If you don't do that, you may end up a year or two from now slapping yourself on the forehead and saying, "What was I thinking?"

When you take off your rose-colored glasses, who are you really looking at? Consider the basic character of this person – is he or she someone you respect? Can you live with the values this person exhibits? Is he or she kind or mean, dishonest or trustworthy, respectful or disrespectful? How does this person treat you? Really explore this one long and hard, and if you can't answer the question, then ask a friend you trust to tell you what he or she sees. How does this person treat, and talk about, people in service positions – the grocery store clerk, the waiter, the mailman, or the garbage collector? How about financially – is this person a spender or saver? Does this person want kids or not? What are his or her ambitions, goals, and dreams?

I could keep going, but I think you are getting the idea. Look closely at the person you are beginning to get attached to and be honest with yourself about these things. Ask yourself if you can live with this person exactly as he or she is, because many of these traits won't change. They may evolve, but it could be for better or worse. And remember, your partner is not a home improvement project, so you either like the person he or she is or you cut your losses and look elsewhere.

Enjoy the dating process, but don't be blind to the real person you are dating. It will save you years of heartache, and maybe even divorce, if you do a thorough screening now.

Your Action Step: If you're currently dating, run your partner through the above list and see what happens. If you aren't dating, run yourself through the list – are you living your life in alignment with who you really want to be?

Chapter 45

New Year, New Day

I love January 1st every year. It always feels like someone came along and wiped my slate clean and I get to start fresh. I wake up with a sense of hope and newness, ready to accept whatever was and embark on a new path – one that seems more directed, more optimistic, and more conquerable.

How about if you lived your dating life like this and made every date a chance to start fresh – out with the old and in with the new?

Make time to get rid of:

O –   overused, ineffective thoughts, patterns and actions
L –   lame excuses
D –   dysfunctional behaviors, situations and people

And bring in:

N –   nice. Be nice to yourself, be nice to others – give people a chance and give yourself a break.
E –   empower your dreams. Go for what makes your heart sing and your soul smile. Stop settling for less.
W –   why not me? You have dreams – do you believe in your ability to make those dreams happen?

Think of it this way: most likely what you are dreaming of has been accomplished by someone else in some capacity, so if they can do it, YOU CAN DO IT. Make it your daily mantra to say,

"Why not me?" When people say you can't do something, smile and say, "Why not me?" – then leave before they bombard you with all their fears and pessimism.

With each day and each dating opportunity, you can start fresh, and I encourage you to do that. I also encourage you to look at how the OLD patterns in your life currently affect your attitude, your actions, and/or your dating abilities and do some work around it. Think of the thoughts that sabotage you; consider all the excuses you use to not do something. Think of the dysfunctional behaviors, situations, and people that surround you and decide how you're going to change your environment. As you clean house on the OLD, you're setting yourself up for the NEW – and exactly what NEW will be is completely up to you. Remember: "*Why not me?*" Go after your life with gusto and with the belief that what you want is absolutely possible.

Your Action Step: Take some time and really assess how the OLD pieces are affecting your life. Do what you can to clean them out of your life, with help if necessary. Contrary to popular but misguided belief, asking for help is not a sign of weakness but rather a sign of a very smart person who wants to move forward in a big way.

❧ Chapter 46 ❧

Become the Person You Want to Attract

One of my favorite quotes from Gandhi is: *"Be the change you wish to see in the world."* It has such an important message for all of us – we must become what it is that we want the world to be. If we want world peace, where can we bring more peace to our daily lives, including having peaceful thoughts?

Now consider this quote in regards to relationships – be the person you wish to attract. If you want someone who is financially responsible – are you financially responsible? Where do you need to make improvements? Do you want someone who doesn't yell or get verbally out of control? How are you doing in this area, and how did you do in past relationships? What about wanting someone who treats you well? How well do you treat yourself and how well do you treat others?

I used to be a party girl – at the time, it was fun! I did, however, come to realize that the men I was attracting were great partiers but not great partners. So I had to stop and ask myself, "Did I really want a great partier or did I want a great partner?" I clearly wanted a great partner. So I toned down the party girl in me and started thinking and acting more like a great partner. Now the party girl still shows up occasionally, but it's more in balance with the person I really want to be on this planet.

It has been proven time and time again that how we live our life draws people who live their life in a similar manner. So consider what it is that's really important to you in relationships, and then ask how you're doing in each area and what you can do to improve in that area.

Your Action Step: Think about one or two qualities that are really important for you to have in a relationship. Then ask yourself how you're living those qualities and where you can make improvements.

✑ Chapter 47 ✑

Negotiables and Non-Negotiables

Have you made your list of qualities you want in a partner? This is one of the most common relationship practices out there, and it serves as a great way to clarify what it is you're really seeking. If you haven't done it, do it now. What is it that you want in a partner? Do you want someone who is kind, loving, affectionate, open, or respectful? Do you want someone with a good sense of humor, a job on Wall Street, or a large extended family? Do you want someone who is an extrovert or an introvert? How about someone who lives in your city or someone who lives in China? Do you want to be with someone who has kids, doesn't have kids, or wants kids? Do you want someone who smokes, is a casual drinker, or a big partier? The possibilities are endless, so have fun creating your list. I have clients with over 100 items on their partner list.

Once you have your list, then mark everything with either Negotiable (I could bend on this one) or Non-Negotiable (I absolutely must have this in a relationship). If your list of non-negotiables is longer than 10 items, then you need to find a way to pare it down so it becomes more achievable. Ask yourself, "What is it about this item that's really non-negotiable?"

On my list, one of my non-negotiables was excessive gambling. There really wasn't anything I wanted to reframe, pare down, or change about it. This one stayed on my list as is. Another one of my non-negotiables was religion. I originally had written down that my partner had to practice the same religion as me, attend church regularly, and live their beliefs. After some deeper thought I came to a broader truth around this item – they had to have some kind of personal relationship with God and they would need to let me live my spiritual life my way. This completely opened up the range of potential partners and was easy to screen for.

This list will help keep you focused on what you want in a partner; just make sure you aren't cutting yourself off from possibilities by being too rigid. People tend to put rigid rules in place when they are afraid they won't be able to stand up for themselves. So practice standing up for your values and what's important to you, and it will be easier to relax those rigid rules and lean into what's possible in relationships.

Your Action Step: Make your list (or review your list), and then honestly and thoroughly go through it. Are you being rigid in an area where you could be flexible? Once you are clearer on that, define each quality and be sure you're living it.

❧ Chapter 48 ❧

Alone vs. Lonely

If you are single, being alone is your current reality. You are alone, as in you are not in an intimate relationship. Singleness does not define you as good or bad; it's simply a statement of where you are in your journey. Lonely is an emotion. Emotions are part of life, and they can either run your life or not.

Since being alone is just a statement of fact and it usually doesn't have an emotional pull to it, then you get to decide if being alone in any given moment is where you want to be or not. If you are the kind of person who relishes alone time, then savor your time alone, because once you're in a relationship this will change. If you are a person who really doesn't enjoy alone time, then get out and be with people – you are in charge of what's unfolding in your life, so take the reins and go socialize.

If you get swept away by the lonely feeling – which happens to just about everyone sometimes – then don't beat yourself up for it; instead, nurture that lonely feeling. Call it what it is and give yourself permission to feel it - maybe journal, take a slow walk, or meditate. Our feelings move out of us much more quickly if we don't fight them. Consider the phrase, "What you resist, persists." So instead, lean into the feeling for a limited amount of time. Acknowledge its presence and just be with it – for fifteen minutes, one hour, or the whole night if necessary. Then set a plan of action for the following morning. Consider what will move you out of the lonely feeling – perhaps going to your favorite coffee shop instead of coffee at home, or calling a friend and scheduling something fun to do. Find something that will empower you – going to the gym, cleaning your house, starting or finishing a project. Remember, your emotions have control over you only when you give them control over you.

Whether you are alone and want company or you are feeling lonely, you do have more power to change it than you might realize. Be proactive, take charge, and empower yourself to make positive changes.

Your Action Step: Assess how you're doing with being alone and feeling lonely. Then commit to making the necessary changes (maybe with help) so you once again feel empowered in your life.

Chapter 49

How Fast Should We Move?

Ah, the age-old question: How fast should a relationship progress from dating to marriage? There are many theories out there and, truth be told, it's completely up to the two of you. But the key here is TWO of you.

Both people need to be on board and okay with the pace of the relationship. Let's say you have a great feeling about someone after the third date – which is fabulous – and you're wondering if it's too soon to talk about marriage. The answer is probably yes; most likely, it's time to talk only about the next step of the relationship. It is critical to give the relationship some time to unfold and flourish. And you also want plenty of time to flush out the truth of who this person is and how they're going to treat you in a variety of situations, and vice versa.

Now, picture yourself two years into the relationship, and no one has talked about your future. Unless you are BOTH happy with being perpetual daters, someone has to be willing to bring up the subject of your future and see if you are even in the same boat.

Neither scenario is ideal. Moving too fast makes it hard to be objective about the person you're dating and to see them without rose-colored glasses. Moving too slow can be an indicator of someone who will never commit or someone who doesn't know if you are the person they want to travel the journey of life with. Just remember, infatuation wears off about six to twelve months into a relationship – the best way to see if you're a good fit with this person is to see how you feel after that period wanes.

Your Action Step: Reflect on your past relationships and ask yourself if you moved too fast or too slow. Make a plan (a flexible one, of course) for how you will handle the speed of your current relationship or your next relationship.

❧ Chapter 50 ❧

Handling Rejection

E very "no" you hear leads you one step closer to the "yes" you are seeking. Don't think about bad dates, complete mismatches, and the lack of sparks as bad things. Instead, consider that you have just moved one step closer to finding your ideal partner.

Rejection can wreak havoc on your self-esteem, and dating can totally feel like rejection. But what if it's really not rejection? Remember, dating is a screening process (for both people) to see if they have enough in common to build a life together, so take rejection out of your vocabulary. When your mind starts trying to convince you that you've been rejected yet again, get firm and perhaps even vocal. Don't give your mind and its running negative dialogue the power to flush your dreams right out of existence. Perhaps this sounds familiar:

> **Rational Mind:** "Hmmm...okay, I have had three dates this month and nothing really came of them. Guess I better keep looking."

> **Negative, Defeatist Mind:** "Keep looking – are you kidding? Three dates and nothing happened? Give it up, go back to bed and resign yourself to being single. There isn't anyone out there that's going to like you. Remember you haven't finished your degree, you are 10 pounds overweight, and you're way too emotional. It's

obvious that if you're going to attract the right partner, you have to be perfect."

When this happens, it's time to get vocal with your defeatist mind and try a new tactic:

Rational, Empowered Mind: "HEY – STOP! I went on three dates; there are thousands of other prospects out there and I'm going to keep looking. And maybe I'm not perfect but, you know what, neither is anyone else. You need to be quiet and stop trying to sabotage my dreams. Now, I'm going to the gym and I'm going to take care of myself and keep my eyes wide open."

We are very quick (trained over years of practice, in fact) to believe whatever our negative mind says to us, and I'm encouraging you to learn to talk back to it. In fact, get forceful with its incessant noise. You would never let a friend talk to you like that, so refuse to take if from yourself.

And remember it's not rejection – it's one step closer to the partner you are seeking!

Your Action Step: Take an inventory of the negative things you say to yourself and, for each one, find a new and empowering way to think about it.

Chapter 51

A Few More Things to Think About

Being single is not a curse – it's the current state of your life. How you handle being single is completely up to you. I can't stress to you enough to enjoy this time in your life because you never know how soon it might change. And besides, if it doesn't change, do you want to have any regrets about how you could have lived your life? Anyone who has experienced a really bad relationship will tell you that being single is better than being in a relationship with the wrong person.

They say that opposites attract; while this can be true and totally exciting during the infatuation stage of dating, after the infatuation wears off, opposites fight and they usually fight a lot. Maybe you would enjoy that kind of relationship – seriously, some people do. Some people thrive on intensity and drama and the make-up sex. If that describes you, then the opposite theory is probably a good one. If you're like me, then drama is not something you want in your life on a daily basis – at least not with your life partner. So look for someone who is more similar to you than different; it will make for a much easier relationship and the two of you together can find other ways to create passion, intensity, and great sex.

Consider what you want in a partner. Consider what you really want for your life, and let yourself dream, and dream big! One of the guiding principles in my life and in my coaching practice is this – if you have a yearning in your heart, you have the ways and means to achieve it. Be optimistic in your dating quest, be happy wherever you are, and enjoy the adventures in this part of your life – you never know how close you are to meeting your partner and how quickly your life could change.

Your Action Step: Ponder the following questions:

- Where could I live life more fully?
- How can I find more joy and satisfaction right where I am?
- Does dating my opposite appeal to me?
- What didn't work in past relationships and how can I do things differently next time?
- What is the true yearning in my heart – what are my deepest wishes and dreams?
- What can I do today to act on those wishes and dreams?

Epilogue:
Parting Words of Wisdom for Everyone

The intention of this book was to inspire you and give you new tools for making your relationships work even better. As you practice the things you've learned, just remember that you will make mistakes along the way. It's okay – honestly, that's how we learn. Remember when you learned to roller-skate or ride a bike? The first time you attempted it, you probably weren't very good (I know I wasn't). As you kept at it, each moment got better and better until you were proficient. The same will be true with these new relationship skills. The more you practice, the more proficient you will be and the more these thoughts, ideas, and skills will flow naturally.

Take note that the skills you use in one relationship will be effective in other relationships as well. I've found that it can be common in work situations to preface big conversations. Many executives do this naturally. Transfer that skill to dealing with a life partner or your kids and watch what happens. I often treat my kids' questions as explorations in life; well, imagine if I treated all questions this way. I would be gentler and kinder to everyone I encountered, not just my kids. So think about which relationships are easy and ask yourself what makes them easy. Take note of any skills being used that could support your other relationships.

And lastly, believe in yourself as you step out of your comfort zone and practice these new ideas. It takes courage to even admit that you don't have all the answers or that your relationships aren't as fulfilling as you want them to be. Remember that you've started down this path because you want healthier, happier, more loving relationships; don't be derailed because it gets a little hard sometimes. Instead, make that the motivation to keep going until your relationships are flourishing.

Success is the sum of small efforts, repeated day in and day out....
~Robert Collier

Life is a succession of lessons
which must be lived to be understood.
~Ralph Waldo Emerson

About the Author

The majestic Colorado Rocky Mountains are home to Jerilyn Thiel. She was born and raised there, and is currently living in the suburbs of Denver. She was married in 1990 to the love of her life, Greg, and has two wonderful children, Amber and Tyler. In addition to a passion for understanding relationship dynamics, Jerilyn also enjoys cooking, reading, being in nature, laughing, and travel.

Jerilyn grew up in a family that didn't always know how to create healthy relationships, but they did know how to love. She has taken that love and channeled it into a passion for serving others in the area of Life Coaching and Relationship Mentoring. She is a Professional Certified Coach (PCC) with the International Coach Federation; a Certified Fearless Living Coach, Level IV, with the Fearless Living Institute; and a Licensed Spiritual Coach.

Her work as a coach and workshop facilitator centers around supporting people in figuring out where they need to make changes in order to have richer and more fulfilling relationships. She encourages each client to open their hearts, to let go of old patterns and old hurts, to learn new skills, and to have patience and compassion as they grow and change. Jerilyn is dedicated to creating more love on the planet, one relationship at a time.

For more information about coaching or mentoring with Jerilyn, upcoming seminars or teleclasses, and ordering additional copies of this book; please visit www.YourPossibilities.com, email Jerilyn at Jerilyn@YourPossibilities.com, or call 720-283-0532.

❧ Testimonials for Jerilyn's Work ❧

Our lives and our marriage were in deep trouble. Individually we were losing ourselves and we had nothing left for the union. We found, and went into, the most effective, caring "therapy" on the planet. Jerilyn's no BS techniques were cushioned with this magnificent well of compassion. She very carefully directed us through a very difficult time in our lives. It was truly a cross roads, it was clear we had a 50-50 chance to save our marriage. The bonus was; we did save our marriage, salvaged, grew and blossomed our own individualities. In fact, Jerilyn's coaching impact led my husband to a new career path. He was trained in the art of business communication as a part of his manager's training but this took it to a whole new level when he started using the tools we learned from Jerilyn: Wow!

Denise Rolen; Owner, Network for Health

Gregg Oliver; Principal, Pathfinder Communication

San Diego, CA

Jerilyn is a gem. Over the last few years, I've had the honor of attending several workshops facilitated by Jerilyn, as well as participating in numerous teleclasses that she was teaching. Brimming with compassion, Jerilyn is kind and gentle and yet also extraordinarily honest and direct when necessary. She has an amazing way of cutting through the complicated layers of confusion that we all feel sometimes, especially with issues involving relationships, and moving right to the heart of the matter with wisdom and clarity. Jerilyn brings a joyfulness to her teaching that is infectious and she shows you how to bring that same joyfulness to your own relationships, be them romantic or otherwise. Jerilyn has played a big role in showing me how to establish and nurture relationships in my life that are more loving, healthy, well-balanced, and, above all else, happy.

C. T.; Corporate Lawyer

New York, NY

With a loving, passionate, and nurturing spirit, Jerilyn is masterful in using solid, foundational skills to bring out the inner brilliance in each person she touches. As my personal life coach and coaching program mentor, Jerilyn supported me in learning what it truly means to invest in all of my relationships, beginning with the relationship I have with myself. She guided me through the greatest relationship challenges of my life, helping me to become fully acquainted with my own heart. I would not have been as successful in my coaching program or in my present day relationships without Jerilyn's love, support, and wisdom! Jerilyn is a gift to everyone who is lucky enough to work with her.

Aubrey Hill

Life Coach, Teaching Mentor

Jerilyn has a unique way of seeing the world. She is clear and filled with hope. She brings a warmth and depth to the world that is unique. Over the years Jerilyn has walked with me through some experiences that are far beyond my words and what I ever thought I could get through. During the intense pain of loss and letting go of my son, Jerilyn was able to keep reminding me of what was truth. She asked me over and over what is the truth as I would begin to beat myself up in the tangled grief. She helped me remember what was beautiful about my son and walked with me as I grieved it all. When I couldn't find the light Jerilyn pointed out a new possibility and new perspective. Jerilyn is brilliant in what she does. She knows the power of truth and kindness. Her wisdom is a life time gift.

C. A. S.

MA, Counseling and Psychological Services